FROM THE

HEART

OF THE

CROW

COUNTRY

FROM THE

HEART

OF THE

CROW

COUNTRY

The Crow Indians' Own Stories

JOSEPH MEDICINE CROW

THE LIBRARY OF THE AMERICAN INDIAN

HERMAN J. VIOLA, EDITOR

CROWN TRADE PAPERBACKS
New York

The editors and publishers would especially like to thank Jan Danis for her invaluable help in making this book a reality. Her skill and dedication are greatly appreciated.

Published by Crown Trade Paperbacks, 201 East 50th Street, New York, New York 10022. Member of the Crown Publishing Group.

Random House, Inc. New York, Toronto, London, Sydney, Auckland

Originally published by Orion Books in 1992.
CROWN TRADE PAPERBACKS and colophon are trademarks of Crown Publishers, Inc.

Manufactured in the United States of America

Design by Leonard Henderson

Library of Congress Cataloging-in-Publication Data
Medicine Crow, Joseph, 1913–
    From the heart of the Crow country : the Crow Indians' own stories
    / Joseph Medicine Crow.
        p. cm. — (The Library of the American Indian)
    Originally published: 1st ed. New York : Orion Books. c1992.
    Includes Index.
    1. Crow Indians—History. 2. Crow Indians—Folklore. I. Title.
    II. Series.
    [E99.C92M43 1994]
    973'.04975—dc20   94-9656
                                    CIP

ISBN 0-517-88220-5
10 9 8 7 6 5 4 3 2 1
First Paperback Edition

Contents

≈≈≈≈≈≈≈≈≈≈≈≈≈≈

CONTENTS

Foreword

Joseph Medicine Crow is one of the best-known storytellers of the Crow Indian tribe of Montana. I first met him in the spring of 1973, in my role as director of the Smithsonian Institution's National Anthropological Archives. The archives is considered one of the world's finest collections of research materials on the Indians of the Americas. It is, in fact if not in name, the "National Archives of the American Indian." Early one morning my boss, Cliff Evans, chairman of the Department of Anthropology, called me to ask a favor. "Herman," he said, "an old fraternity brother from my USC days has shown up unexpectedly, and I am too busy to spend any time with him. He happens to be a Crow Indian, so I'll bet he would love to see some of the historical Crow photographs in your archives. Just spend a few minutes with him and then let him spend the rest of the time looking at old photographs."

A few minutes later Cliff appeared in my office with his fraternity brother in tow. I met a short, stocky, dark-skinned, stern-faced man in cowboy hat and cowboy boots. After my boss left and we exchanged pleasantries, I asked Joe if he wanted to see some Crow pictures. "I would like that," he replied. Leaving him in the research room with a stack of two hundred or so, I returned to my office. From time to time throughout the morning I walked past him and noticed that he appeared to be examining the old photographs with intense interest. As he neared the end of the pile, I asked him what he thought of the pictures. "They are very interesting," he said, "but I must say I am disappointed in them."

"Why?" I asked with some surprise.

"Because you don't have a picture of my grandmother here!" As I started to explain that we could not be expected to have a picture of every Indian who ever lived—it turned out his grandmother lived to be a hundred and five and could speak five languages—he continued his examination of the remaining pictures and then stopped with a look of utter amazement on his face.

"What's the problem?" I asked.

"This cannot exist. I never saw it before." The photograph was of a handsome man and woman with two young boys. "That is my mother and father and brothers," Joe explained. Eventually, it turned out that the picture had been taken in Washington in the 1920s when a group of Crows came to the capital as part of a Shriners' rodeo. Joe recalled that he had chosen to remain on the reservation that summer, preferring hunting and fishing to traveling. One of the boys had later died, but his parents, now in their late seventies, were still alive, so Joe asked for a copy of the picture to give to his mother. Thus began my friendship with one of the most remarkable and unusual people I have ever met.

If this were Japan, Joseph Medicine Crow would be a living cultural treasure, for he is a unique individual by anyone's standards. The first member of the Crow tribe to graduate from college—Bacone—and the first to obtain a master's degree (in anthropology at the University of Southern California), he was working on his doctorate in anthropology before World War II interrupted his studies. Although offered a commission because of his college background, he refused on the grounds that a warrior must first prove himself in battle before becoming a leader of men—the "worst mistake I ever made," he admits, "because the U.S. Army didn't work on the principles of the Crow tribe and I never got another chance at a commission."

No matter. Descended from a long and famous line of Crow war chiefs, Private Medicine Crow went on to distinguish himself on the battlefields of Europe, where he counted coup on the enemy and even captured a German horse. Yet it is his gift as a storyteller, the carrier of his people's oral history, which makes his contributions to the Library of the American Indian so special and significant.

What makes his work especially valuable is the fact that, as a scholar as well as a storyteller, he understands the strengths and weaknesses of both oral and recorded history. Where possible he has always tried to verify stories he has learned from other participants, witnesses, and archival and printed records.

I came to appreciate Joe more and more during my many visits to his beloved Crow country. Thanks to Joe, after each visit I would come away with a better appreciation for the Crow people and their place in American history. He showed me some of the special places in Crow country—

the mountain ledges where Crow boys over the centuries sought their vision quests, the gap in the Pryor Mountains where Crow war parties on their way to meet their Sioux and Cheyenne enemies would leave stone offerings to the "little people" as a token of respect, and, of course, the Little Bighorn River where his great-uncle, White-Man Runs Him, gained a piece of immortality along with George Armstrong Custer, who refused to believe his Crow scouts when they told him that there were too many Sioux for the Seventh Cavalry to face that fateful day in 1876.

The traditional Crow country is a vast area that stretches across much of present-day Wyoming and Montana. Today, because of several treaties negotiated with a government that somehow forgot that the Crows were always the friend of the white man, Crow country is very much reduced in size, but the reservation is still, by any measure, a large and wonderful tract of land that dominates the southeast corner of Montana. Its lush meadows and wooded hills still abound with game. Once ideal buffalo country, today its pastures fatten the horses that remain so much a part of Crow life as well as vast herds of beef cattle that now graze where buffaloes once roamed.

The Crows believe their country is the best place on earth, a gift to them from the First Maker, who created the world and then divided it among the various people who came to inhabit it. Their country is neither too hot in summer, nor too cold in winter. It has beautiful mountains, many lakes and rivers filled with clear, cold water, and early on it had buffalo and other wildlife in numbers that defied counting. But the Crows knew that the First Maker had a purpose in giving them such a favored location. He wished to test their courage, so he surrounded them with several of the most numerous, fearsome, and militant tribes on the Northern

Plains. As a result, generation after generation of outnumbered Crow warriors had to defend their homeland against incursions from Sioux, Cheyenne, and Blackfeet war parties intent on capturing their splendid horses and their beautiful women. Constant warfare made the Crows a brave and hardy people. It also explains why they befriended the white man and served as allies in the various battles between the U.S. Cavalry and their Sioux and Cheyenne enemies, culminating in the Battle of the Little Bighorn.

Now nearly eighty years old, Joseph Medicine Crow is the acknowledged historian of the Crow tribe. Throughout his life he has collected the stories of his people, beginning with those of his own family. One of his grandfathers, for whom he is named, was Medicine Crow, one of the tribe's last war chiefs and a signer of the 1880 treaty with the United States. A great-uncle, White-Man Runs Him, was not only Custer's favorite Crow scout, but also the one who lived the longest. The old man lived in Joe's home on the reservation, and from him Joe heard many stories about the Indian wars. Because of his role in the Custer fight, many white historians also came to listen to the old man's stories, but eventually he stopped talking to them because of their disbelief at some of the things he said, especially the notion that members of the Seventh Cavalry drank whiskey before going into battle.

Fascinated by the tales of his grandfathers, Joe Medicine Crow began collecting stories of the other elderly Crows as well as members of other tribes, including their traditional enemies, the Sioux and Cheyenne. The Northern Cheyenne Reservation, in fact, adjoins the Crow Reservation, and as the bitterness that lingered from the old days began to disappear, Joe made several close friends on that reservation, always seeking out the storytellers, the carriers of traditional culture, especially those old people who could tell him about life before the reservation, when the Crows, the Sioux, and the Cheyenne were free peoples who followed the buffalo and lived as their fathers had lived.

Joe Medicine Crow still collects stories, but, as he points out, "the traditional historians and storytellers are all gone now and I must work with their children and grandchildren, who have been exposed to their views and recitals of the old stories."

By combining oral tradition and the written record, Joseph Medicine Crow has compiled a knowledge of the history of the Northern Plains tribes that is unique in the American Indian community. Few Native Americans alive today can provide such a compelling and authentic window into a way of life that ended more than a century ago. *From the Heart of the Crow Country* is his first book.

—*Herman J. Viola*

Preface

~~~~~~~~~~~~~~~~~~~~~~~~~~~~

At the outset I wish to make a specific statement, my position statement as it were, as a historian of the Crow tribe. I was designated as the tribal historian and anthropologist by the Crow Tribal Council in 1948. I have always endeavored to conduct my researches in the following manner:

1. I try to keep my tribal ethnohistory data as accurate and current as possible through constant checking, rechecking, and cross-checking of the documents accumulated on the particular project I am pursuing. Unfortunately, the professional tribal historians and storytellers are all gone now and I must work with their children and grandchildren who have been exposed to their views and recitals of the old stories. Working with these secondhand informants is like putting a jigsaw puzzle together, but it has been interesting and challenging. But thanks to ethnographer-investigators such

as Edward Curtis, William Wilschutt, and Robert Lowie and historians such as James Bradley, Frank Linderman, Thomas B. Marquis, and so on, many of the stories and history told by the old Crow historians have been recorded on paper and film.

2. I cross-check and try to corroborate these native accounts with outside sources of information, such as the written memoirs, diaries, reports, and notes of the white men who came into contact with the tribes well in advance of the expanding western civilization in the New World. The first of these newcomers were the fur traders, trappers, and adventurers; later came the missionaries, gold miners, the military, settlers going to Oregon and California, and others. Reading the stories told by such colorful early mountain men as Jim Bridger, John Colter, and Jim Beckwourth is quite an adventure. Even serious and astute researchers can be led off on wild tangents into fairy-tale land. Separating the real from the yarn, the ordinary from the dramatic, and the possible from the impossible in these accounts of early Indian-white relationships is a trying experience. And to make matters even worse and more confusing is the exaggerated work of latter-day fiction writers, rehash authors of Western history, and television scriptwriters who have been creating characters more colorful than the real ones. Today, we read paperbacks and see screen characters like Jeremiah Johnson, the Man Called Horse, Grizzly Adams, and others who make Jim Bridger and Jim Beckwourth look like Sunday-school boys in knee pants.

3. I also depend a great deal on the archaeologists who study the past life of Indians through their excavation of sites of habitation and other activities. I must admit that their reports are often difficult to read and understand, but I generally find corroborative evidence from this science to

support and bolster my researches and findings into the ethnohistory of my own tribe, as well as of others. Here also the researcher must be on guard, as archaeologists are human and they often come up with conflicting and contradictory interpretations and concepts.

After I have gone through these three steps in a particular project, I then synthesize my findings and try to come forward with a logical conclusion. But I usually state that the conclusion is not necessarily final and is always subject to modification pending future discovery of new data.

The "Crow Migration Story" was presented at the 1979 annual meeting of the Montana Archaeological Society; an earlier version of "Crow Indian Buffalo Jumps" appeared in the *Plains Anthropologist* 23 (November 1978); the biographical sketch "Medicine Crow" was published by the Crow Central Education Commission (Crow Agency, Montana, 1979).

To the best of my recollections I am listing here the names of Crows who have served as informants in my tribal researches since 1932. As to dates, places, and other details of my interviews, these are lost in time. Prior to 1932 I made no notes of any kind. In my early boyhood, it was my good fortune to have known many pre-reservation Crows, including my four grandparents. Both my grandfathers, Medicine Crow and Yellowtail, were ceremonial traditionalists and often invited their fellow men to sweat baths. At such times many stories were told. I would sit quietly and listen. To this day I still recall the many stories told by such men as Chief Flathead Woman, Chief Around His Neck, White-Man Runs Him, White Arm, and many others whose names I can no longer recall.

Since I began recording stories and collecting data on

Crow culture in 1932, I have personally interviewed from time to time the following elders of the tribe:

1. In 1932 Cold Wind, a little more than ninety, told me in detail the stories of the separation of the Crow and Hidatsa tribes and of the long migrations of the Crow people.

2. Yellowbrow, who died in the mid-1940s at about eighty years of age, told me bits of Crow history, especially about warfare with other tribes.

3. Plain Feather, who died about 1970 at age one hundred, was my most dedicated and prolific informant. He was trained as a historian by his uncle, Chief Iron Bull, who was himself a good historian. Plain Feather was good on any subject, even the genealogy of individuals and families.

4. Charles Ten Bear, who died in the mid-1960s when more than eighty, was good in reciting accounts of tribal wars.

5. My maternal grandmother, Lizzie Chienne Yellowtail, who died in 1969 at one hundred and five, was not a great storyteller. But when urged, she would come up with bits of good information about Crow history and ethnology.

6. Mary Chienne Takes Gun, Lizzie's younger sister who died in the early 1960s when about eighty-eight years old, had an astonishing memory. She and my grandmother were only one-quarter Indian, but they knew Crow history and culture. Mary was a good and true medicine woman. I took her life story and hope to publish it.

7. Medicine Sheep was my paternal grandmother. She died in 1948 at the age of ninety-eight. She was good at recalling early reservation life in Livingston, Absarokee, and Lodge Grass. She was the wife of Chief Medicine Crow, who was suddenly thrown into the "civilization pot" after 1870.

8. White-Man Runs Him, the brother of my grandmother Medicine Sheep, was good on the Custer campaign and battle. He was one of Custer's six Crow scouts.

The following informants were first-generation reservation Crows. Many were sent to off-reservation schools such as Carlisle, Haskell, and Sherman Institute, and they came back well educated. Many became tribal leaders after the old reservation chiefs, among them my grandfather, retired.

1. Frank Shively, a Carlisle graduate, was a half-blood Crow. He came back from school in the early 1900s and became involved in tribal affairs with the federal government, the state of Montana, the cattle industry, and other entities that wanted to open the Crow Reservation to whites. He died an old man in the mid-1940s. He was a good informant on Crow-white marriages and the genealogy of such families.

2. Thomas Asa Laforge was another educated half-blood Crow. He was good on Crow history since the establishment of the reservation. He received much information from his father, Thomas H. Laforge, the white Crow Indian of the book by Thomas B. Marquis. Incidentally, I knew Thomas H. Laforge quite well, as he lived with his daughter Mary Little Nest during his last years. Mr. Little Nest was the brother of my grandfather Medicine Crow.

3. James Carpenter, another educated half-blood Crow, was a politician all his life and was well versed in the political attempts by Montana congressmen and senators to open the reservation to whites. Mr. Carpenter turned his papers over to me before he died, just before World War II.

4. George Washington Hogan was the brother of my grandmother Lizzie Chienne Yellowtail. He graduated from

Carlisle in the early 1900s and was also a tribal political figure until he died in the late 1960s when about eighty. He too fought against opening the Crow Reservation. His writings on Crow history were lost after his death, but I received a great deal of information from him.

5. Carl Crooked Arm died in the early 1970s when he was about eighty. He received his formal education from Haskell Institute in Kansas. His knowledge of Crow history came from his father, Chief Crooked Arm. Carl was a wonderful storyteller, and I was his favorite listener.

6. Joseph Rockabove was middle-age when he died in 1976. His grandfather was a tribal historian who could trace his genealogy back to the day so long ago when Chief No Vitals led his secessionist group out of the Hidatsa country. Joseph would say that he was the fifteenth generation since the separation. He had a good memory and could recall the stories told by his grandfather.

Today I rely on the sons and grandchildren of these old storytellers for confirmation of bits of stories and information I had heard as a boy. George Bulltail of Pryor, Montana, has been a great help. Before he died in the early 1980s, I conferred with him often, because he too relied on his recollections of what he had heard from the old storytellers.

Mary Takes Gun Old Coyote, now about one hundred years of age, is the daughter of Mary Chienne Takes Gun. Mary is the best source of information available today. She is good with history and Crow ethnology and equally good with tribal ceremonials and social customs.

Robert Yellowtail died at the age of one hundred in June 1989. He was the oldest Crow at the time. He was a cousin to Mary Takes Gun Old Coyote, presently the oldest living Crow. Robert was one of the first scholars of the Crow tribe.

He graduated from Sherman Institute in Riverside, California, and studied law in Los Angeles. He with Shively, Carpenter, and others fought off all attempts to open the Crow Indian Reservation to the public since 1905. Mr. Yellowtail knew all about the stormy political history of the Crow tribe.

Over the years I have also used several non-Indian informants, such as old-time cowboys Matt Tschirgi, Ray Powers, Har Willcutt, Bill Bowman, and Slim Kobold. They came and worked for various cattle outfits leasing Crow Reservation range lands. I also worked with the late Western artist Ken Ralston, who was a fine historian as well as a painter. Hans Kleiber was also a good friend of mine.

For my present archaeological researches I am now working with Dr. Les Davis of the Museum of the Rockies, Bozeman, Montana; Dr. Lawrence Lorendorf and Dr. Richard Fox, both from the University of North Dakota; and Stuart Conner of Billings, Montana, who perhaps knows more about Indian rock writing (rock art) than anyone I know.

Dr. Herman Viola, formerly chief of the National Anthropological Archives, Smithsonian Institution, has been very helpful in providing me with historical data on Indians in general and Crow Indians in particular.

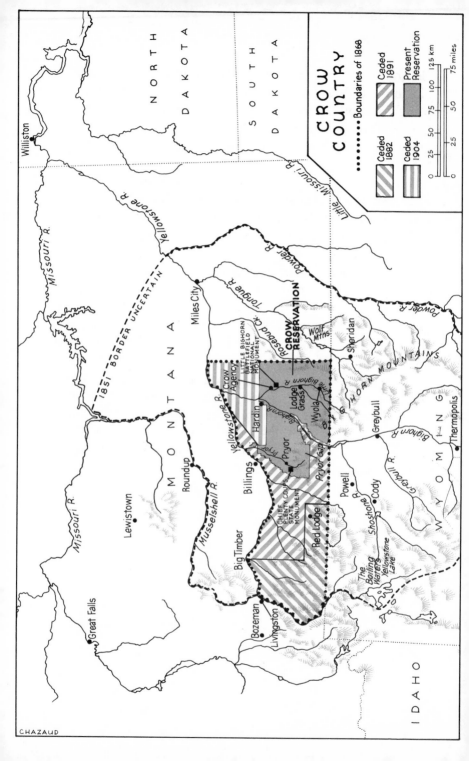

The Crow Country

An Epigraph

The Crow country is a good country. The Great Spirit has put it exactly in the right place; while you are in it you fare well; whenever you go out of it, whichever way you travel, you will fare worse.

If you go to the south, there you have to wander over great barren plains; the water is warm and bad, and you meet the fever and ague.

To the north it is cold; the winters are long and bitter, and no grass; you cannot keep horses there, but must travel with dogs. What is a country without horses!

On the Columbia they are poor and dirty, paddle about in canoes, and eat fish. Their teeth are worn out; they are always taking fishbones out of their mouths. Fish is poor food.

To the east, they dwell in villages; they live well; but they drink the muddy water of the Missouri—that is bad. A Crow's dog would not drink such water.

About the forks of the Missouri is a fine country; good water; good grass; plenty of buffalo. In summer, it is almost as good as the Crow country: but in winter it is cold; the grass is gone; and there is no salt weed for the horses.

The Crow country is exactly in the right place. It has snowy mountains and sunny plains; all kinds of climates and good things for every season. When the summer heats scorch the prairies, you can draw up under the mountains, where the air is sweet and cool, the grass fresh, and the bright streams come tumbling out of the snow banks. There you can hunt the elk, the deer, and the antelope, when their skins are fit for dressing; there you will find plenty of white bears and mountain sheep.

In the autumn, when your horses are fat and strong from the mountain pastures, you can go down into the plains and hunt the buffalo, or trap beaver on the streams. And when winter comes on, you can take shelter in the woody bottoms along the rivers; there you will find buffalo meat for your-selves, and cottonwood bark for your horses: or you may winter in the Wind River valley, where there is salt weed in abundance.

The Crow country is exactly in the right place. Every-thing good is to be found there. There is no country like the Crow country.

—Arapooish, a Crow chief,
to Mr. Robert Campbell
of the Rocky Mountain Fur Company,
as recounted by Washington Irving
in *The Adventures of Captain Bonneville*

The Crow Indians

~~~~~~~~~~~~~~~~~~~~

EARLY HISTORY

Most of the Northwest Plains Indians originally came from northeastern North America. They were forced out of their forest and woodland habitat by more numerous and powerful tribes, perhaps the Chippewa, Ojibwa, and Cree. The ancestors of the present Crow Indians came from a "Land of Many Lakes," probably in the headwaters of the Mississippi or farther north in the Winnepa Lake region, in the latter part of the sixteenth century. Legends also refer to an ancient ancestral tribe that once lived in the woodlands of what is now the state of Wisconsin about 1500 A.D. This tribe migrated westward across the Mississippi River looking for buffalo. They eventually settled along the Missouri River in what is now North and South Dakota. These people lived in semipermanent villages of lodges covered with earth. They became known as the "People Who Lived in Earthen Lodges."

Nearly four hundred years ago (ca. 1600–25) these people divided into two factions. One group migrated west and eventually claimed most of what is now eastern Montana and northern Wyoming as its homeland. At the time of the separation, this group numbered about four hundred. Its population reached about eight thousand before the smallpox epidemic of the middle 1800s. Known then as the Absarokee, the Crow tribe traveled in two or three groups or bands.

In the Hidatsa language, Absarokee means "Children of the Large-beaked Bird" (*absa* meaning "large-beaked bird" and *rokee* meaning "children" or offspring). Other Indian tribes called these people the "Sharp People," implying that they were as crafty and alert as the bird *absa* (probably the raven) for which they were named. In referring to them in the hand-sign language, they would simulate the flapping of bird wings in flight. White men interpreted this sign to mean the bird *crow* and thus called the tribe the "Crow Indians."

RECENT HISTORY

Before the Lewis and Clark expedition through Crow country in 1805–6, very few white men had ever seen the Absarokee or Crow Indians. In 1743 the La Vérendryes brothers had ventured from their Canadian frontier outpost and visited the Crow country, naming the inhabitants the "Handsome Men" (*Beaux Hommes*). After Lewis and Clark, various fur companies and their trappers moved into Crow country. Trading posts were built—Fort Lisa at the junction of the Yellowstone and Bighorn rivers in 1807, Fort Cass further up the Bighorn, and others.

By 1864 the Bozeman Trail, the well-traveled emigrant route, was blazed right through the Crow country. Shortly thereafter, three military posts—Fort Reno, Fort Phil Kearney, and Fort C. F. Smith—were constructed along the trail to protect the emigrants on their way to the gold mines of western Montana. The Sioux Indians, who were forced out of their Black Hills country, came to this area to continue their resistance against the white invasion and forced the government to abandon these forts. Fort C. F. Smith was considered the most dangerous post of the frontier; it was abandoned by the Army less than two years after it was established.

RELATIONS WITH THE UNITED STATES

In 1825 the Crow tribe and the United States signed a treaty of friendship. In 1851 the so-called Fort Laramie Treaty established the boundaries of the "Indian Country" for several tribes, including an area of 35,531,147 acres for the Crow Indians. This was followed by another Fort Laramie treaty in 1868, which reduced the Crow country to 8,000,400 acres.

An act of Congress in 1882 resulted in further reduction of the land, and as compensation the government was to build houses for the Crows and buy livestock for them. By this time the tribe had been settled within the boundaries of the reservation for about ten years. In 1890 more land was ceded to the government, for which the Crows received $940,000. In 1905 the last large cession was made, leaving about 2.5 million acres of land for the tribe.

The Crow Indians always felt that the government had failed to give adequate compensation for the land it acquired, estimating that they received less than five cents per acre. In 1904 the Crow tribe first initiated legal proceedings by suing the government for just compensation for lands taken. In 1962 the Court of Indian Claims finally awarded $10,242,984.70 to the Crow Indians.

After 1905 further attempts were made to reduce the Crow Reservation. Senator Dixon in 1910, Senator Meyers in 1915, and Senator Walsh in 1917 each sponsored legislation in Congress to open the balance of the Crow Reservation for settlement by the public, but all attempts failed. On June 4, 1920, Congress passed an act, sponsored by the tribe itself, dividing the remainder of the reservation into tracts that were allotted to every enrolled member of the tribe. The rough mountain areas were withheld from allotment and remained in tribal ownership. The titles to these lands are held in trust by the federal government, and allottees may not dispose of their property without the consent and approval of the government.

PATTERNS OF ABSAROKEE CULTURE

The Absarokee tribe evolved through several stages of cultural development. The early ancestors who lived in the eastern forests practiced agriculture and achieved a fairly high level of civilization. As they were pushed and forced westward into the wilderness, they gradually became more and more dependent on the hunt. By the time of their settlement in the west, their agriculture was limited to the planting of corn and squash.

Soon after their separation from the main tribe, the Absarokee abandoned agricultural ways and became a nomadic people. They were always on the move after game and in constant warfare with other tribes of the Plains and mountains. This pattern of culture came to an end in 1870 when reservation life began.

SOCIAL ORGANIZATION

The family was the primary unit of social organization, and what may be regarded as the secondary unit was the clan. A clan is composed of distantly related families, with membership determined through the mother. A person belongs to his or her mother's clan, not the father's clan. As the tribe increased in population, it divided into subtribes or bands for convenience and travel.

The bands were governed by band chiefs supported by a body of other chieftains as advisers. They managed the affairs of the tribe in matters of hunting, warfare with other tribes, enactments of important ceremonials, and maintenance of law and order. The Crow tribe consisted of two main bands—the River Crows, who lived along the Missouri, Milk, and Yellowstone rivers, and the Mountain Crows, who enjoyed life along the high ranges of northern Wyoming and southern Montana. A third group—known as the Kicked in the Bellies—was closely related to the Mountain Crows. Both large groups had the same clans, there being about twelve, such as the Whistling Waters, Newly Made Lodge Owners, Greasy Mouths, Filth Eaters, and Large Lodges.

Today, the family is still the primary unit of modern Crow society, while the clan is becoming more and more obsolete. The wife's position in the family has become more important than the husband's, whereas in the old days the husband's position was very strong; he enjoyed a double standard to the point that he could have several wives if he wanted.

The affairs of the tribe are now largely administered by the Bureau of Indian Affairs of the federal government. The tribe has a council that runs on a "town meeting" basis. All adults are members of the council. Administrative functions and major undertakings must be approved by officials of the Bureau of Indian Affairs. In 1973 the Indian Self-Determination Act was designed to give tribes more voice in the administration of their affairs.

As citizens of the United States, the Crow Indians, like all Indian tribes, are subject to both state and federal laws, with the same rights and responsibilities as other citizens. The tribe also maintains a structure of law and order within the reservation to deal with problems and situations peculiar to Indian customs and ways that are not covered by state or federal laws. The enforcement of these reservation laws is in the hands of a modern tribal police and court system.

MILITARY ORGANIZATION

In the old days, the many tribes of the Northwest Plains were constantly at war. The cultural pattern of the Crow tribe was therefore definitely militaristic. A man's social prestige depended on his military record. The search for military prowess led to religious experiences and dedications. A warrior was required to complete four difficult war deeds, each at the risk of his life, in order to become a chief.

To the Absarokee, war was not waged for conquest and gain of property or territory; warfare was sport—truly a game of wits, chivalry, bravery, and honor between tribes. In the Crow tribe there were many military clubs and societies that aspiring young warriors sought to join. The tribe and bands were ruled by retired war chiefs with the assistance of these military societies. During World War II some of them were revived, with membership made up of servicemen and veterans who received military names and war songs in accordance with the old customs of these societies.

RELIGIOUS ORGANIZATION

The old-time Crow Indians recognized a supreme being whom they called First Maker, but they did not worship it directly. They sought its benevolence and favor through devotion to various animals and objects of nature that were regarded as possessing supernatural powers given them by the First Maker.

Medicine men, both healers and visionaries, were well versed in the secrets of nature through their intensive study and worship of their respective "gods." They were quite capable of curing various ailments and of coping with unusual situations. People depended on these men for their spiritual guidance and welfare and often joined various religious organizations founded by the medicine men, and yet there was no single prescribed form or method of worship for the entire population. People worshipped their own respective "gods" individually or in small groups as members and participants of a particular ritual or ceremony, such as the Sun Dance, the Sacred Pipe Dance, the Wound Curing Ceremony, and many others.

Today, some of the native religious beliefs and systems of ceremonials have become nearly obsolete, and only a few old people halfheartedly observe them as a matter of habit and form. The Sun Dance and Tobacco Society ceremonials are still quite strong. A fairly large segment of the Crow tribe belongs to the Native American Church, which prescribes the use of peyote, an herb of the cactus family, as its sacrament similarly to the Christian use of bread. In fact, the Native American Church is a hybrid organization with its doctrines and observances based on a combination of Christian ethics and Indian beliefs.

It can be said that, with the exception of comparatively few individuals, nearly all members of the tribe now profess membership in some modern Christian denomination. Since 1886, the Catholics have established and maintained churches and schools on the reservation, as have the Baptists. There are presently four Catholic churches, two Baptist missions, and two Mormon temples on the reservation. In recent years, the Pentecostal, Full Gospel, and other evangelical denominations have become quite active on the Crow and other reservations.

ECONOMIC ORGANIZATION

Prior to reservation life, the Crow economy was based simply on the availability of game and edible plants and the tribe's ability to secure them. Both game and plant foods abounded in the Crow country. Men were responsible only for the hunting of game, while women cured (i.e., dried or smoked) the meats and also gathered roots and berries and prepared them as supplies. Women also manufactured clothes and household equipment and prepared buffalo skins into tepees.

All this has changed, of course, and today Crow Indians live in the same economic system as everyone else. The basis of a Crow's economy and income is his reservation land, which he uses directly as a farmer or livestock operator and indirectly as a landlord or lessor. Many members of the tribe are employed in the government's Bureau of Indian Affairs and in other federally funded programs. The U.S. Indian Health Service and the tribe itself also employ many members.

Occasionally, tribal funds derived from timber sales, grazing land rentals, and mineral leases (oil and coal) are distributed on a per capita basis. Such royalties are not outright payments of money to Indians by the government, as some people believe. During the summer months, some men find employment on ranches, but, as a rule, there are limited employment opportunities on the Crow Reservation. A few find regular employment off the reservation in the coal-mining industry.

The Crow Indian Reservation is located southeast of Billings, Montana. Nearly 2.5 million acres of mountains, foothills, and rolling plains lie within the exterior boundaries, as defined in 1885. As of January 1, 1969, the Crow people retained ownership of 1,567,189 acres of the reservation. The remainder had been sold to non-Indians by the allottees between 1922 and 1962. Since that time the Crow tribe has purchased all of the land sold by individual tribal members.

LANGUAGE

Indian languages, like all other languages of the world, have been studied and classified by linguistic stock. The Absarokee language has been classified as one of Siouan stock. It is comparable in style and form to the languages of the Sioux and Hidatsa, but it is very different from the Flathead and Shoshone languages, which represent different linguistic stocks.

In the old days, the tribes of the Northwest Plains, while speaking different languages and dialects, were able to communicate with one another through the use of a common style of hand signs. Contrary to general opinion, not all Indian tribes were able to use this method of communication.

Many Indian languages have been studied and recorded, including the Crow language. Dr. Robert H. Lowie, formerly of the University of California, made a limited study in 1912 and published a brief pamphlet on this language. The Wycliffe Bible Translators are now making a complete study of the language. The purpose is to translate the Bible into a written Crow language. At present the two main public school districts of the reservation have bilingual education programs funded by the federal government.

PHYSICAL APPEARANCE

The old-time Plains Indians—always on the hunt and warpath, first on foot and later on horseback—were athletic in build, generally lean and tall. The Crow Indian is of this type and was distinguished from other tribes by the style of his hair dressing. He wore long braids and high pompadours.

In 1825, a scholarly white man measured many Crow men and found the average height to be around six feet. The women were shorter and stockily built but were still relatively tall.

MANNER OF DRESS

The Crow Indians, prior to contact with white men, wore clothes of tanned deer, elk, antelope, and buffalo skins for both everyday and dress wear. Dress clothing, worn in dances and ceremonials, were decorated with various ornaments of feathers, seeds, skins of small animals, and shells. Brightly dyed porcupine quills were embroidered into the buckskin clothes.

During the hot summer weather, men generally wore only breechcloths and moccasins, while women and girls wore full dresses at all times. The exposure of any part of a female's body, except for the hands and face, was considered indecent.

Today, Crow Indians wear old-style costumes only at dances and ceremonials and special appearances for the general public. For everyday clothes, they wear typical non-Indian apparel. Very few old men wear moccasins and long braids. Most of the older women still wear their hair in long braids, wear moccasins, and use shawls or blankets (Pendleton) and bright mufflers on their heads. The schoolgirls never wear "Indian" clothes, except on special occasions.

CAMP ACTIVITIES—RECREATION, SPORTS, AND SOCIALS

During periods of respite from the demands of hunting and warfare, the old-time Absarokee camp was full of festivities such as dances, ceremonials, feasts, games for every age, and athletic sports and events for all. The rigors of nomadic life made these people naturally athletic and they enjoyed sports and games. The boys were subjected to vigorous training in running, swimming, wrestling, archery, tracking, hunting, riding, and other skills. The girls received training in domestic arts.

The Crow children, of course, now attend the public schools for their training and education; their tuition is paid to the school districts by the federal government in accordance with old treaty stipulations. There are three public high schools that Crow children attend, at Hardin, Lodge

Grass, and Pryor, Montana. The Indian boys are usually good athletes and take active parts in the sports programs of these schools.

POPULATION TRENDS

The smallpox scourges of the mid-nineteenth century decimated the Crow population from nearly 8,000 to less than 2,000 by 1870. The sudden change from their accustomed life in the open to sedentary life on the reservation proved unhealthy. Tuberculosis and other modern and foreign diseases for which they had little natural resistance kept the population static. Only in the last thirty years have Crow numbers increased significantly. From a population of about 1,000 in 1851, the tribe increased to 2,383 in 1938 to 2,424 in 1943 to 3,235 in 1953 and to 5,127 in December 1968. The 1976 population was 5,986, and today the population of the Crow tribe is approximately 7,500.

The many and frequent instances of marriage of Indian women to trappers, traders, and settlers in the early years reduced the full-blood strain of the tribe to about 25 percent of the population by the onset of World War I. In recent years the number of full-bloods has decreased rapidly.

SOME IMPORTANT EVENTS IN THE HISTORY OF THE CROW TRIBE

ca. 1500   The ancient ancestors of the Crow Indians lived east of the Mississippi River.

ca. 1580 The ancestral tribe of the present Absarokee and Hidatsa lived in a "Land of Forests and Many Lakes." This tribe migrated westward onto the Plains. On the way, two head chiefs fasted at Devil's Lake in search of guidance from the Great Spirit.

ca. 1600 The tribe settled near the junction of the Knife and Missouri rivers. Some time later, a group continued westward led by Chief No Vitals. This band traveled for many years over a large area and eventually came to what is now south-central Montana by ca. 1700.

ca. 1700–35 The tribe acquired horses from Indians near Great Salt Lake. Horses gave mobility to the Crows, and the tribe soon expanded its sphere of influence and began establishing a vast domain, before other northeastern tribes moved in.

1743 Crows saw white men, perhaps for the first time, near what is now the town of Hardin, Montana. These were the La Vérendryes brothers from Canada, who called the Crows *Beaux Hommes,* or Handsome Men.

1805–6 The Lewis and Clark expedition traveled across Crow country. Clark met the Crows at Pompey's Pillar. Francis Larocque visited the Crows on the Yellowstone about this time.

1825 A treaty of friendship—the first for the tribe—was signed by Chief Long Hair of the Crows and Major O'Fallon of the United States.

1840–50   Smallpox invaded the Crow country. The tribe had reached its height of power in the late 1830s and early 1840s under the leadership of Chief Long Hair. The epidemic reduced the population from more than eight thousand to fewer than one thousand.

1851   Crows participated in the so-called Fort Laramie Treaty under Chief (acting) Big Shadow (often called Big Robert or Big Robber in history books). More than thirty-five million acres were reserved to the Crows.

ca. 1862   Combined forces of the Sioux, Cheyenne, and Arapaho tribes attempted to annihilate the Crows but failed. Crow warriors, outnumbered ten to one, succeeded in turning back the invasion. The battle took place seven miles north of what is now Pryor, Montana.

1868   Crows were again called to another Fort Laramie treaty, where Chief Blackfoot represented the tribe. Crow country was reduced to eight million acres.

1870   Crows were required to report to the diminished portion of Crow country and to assume "reservation life." The first government headquarters or agency for the Crows was located at Mission Creek about five miles east of what is now Livingston, Montana.

1872   The Crow Agency moved to the Rosebud River near what is now Absarokee, Montana.

1882–84   Further land reductions concentrated the tribe in the eastern part of the reservation, and the Crow Agency moved again, this time to its present site.

1958   The Crow tribe sold the Yellowtail Dam site and reservoir area for $2.5 million.

1962   The Court of Indian Claims awarded the Crow tribe $10 million for lands taken away from them by the government in 1851.

The Crow
Migration Story

~~~~~~~~~~~~~~~~~~~~~~~~~~~~

The migration story of the Crow Indians, or Absarokee, is certainly interesting, intriguing, and often frustrating to the researcher. At the outset there exists a time gap, as well as a credibility gap, between the legendary and the real, but as oral and recorded history reach back into the past and begin to support and substantiate the legendary, the gap begins to close and a starting point is finally found from which some continuity can be identified and maintained.

Now, let us hear perhaps the most extensive and dramatic Indian migration story ever told, the one known and told by a succession of sixteen generations of Crow historians, keepers of the tribal annals, and tellers of tales. It is said that in the long, long-ago times, the ancestral tribe of the Hidatsa and Crows once lived toward the east in the "tree country," now believed to be the western end of the Great Lakes, say south of Lake Superior and west of Lake Michigan. Here the tribe followed the lifeways of woodland Indians.

One spring, as the grass was turning green and the deer and buffalo were grazing with relish in the open parks, the rains stopped. Hot winds began blowing continuously, and soon the green earth was parched to brown. The buffalo disappeared. The chiefs held council and an earnest search for the vanished herds was organized. Teams of fourteen men were sent out in all directions. The teams sent to the east soon returned and reported that further search was useless, as no tracks had been found going eastward. The other parties eventually returned without success—all but the team going west.

It was a long time later that this last group returned. When they did, each man was laden with huge packs of jerked buffalo meat. Everyone in the tribe had a little meat to eat. The searchers then reported that their travels had led them far to the west where trees began to thin out and there were open areas of grassland. There the hills were rolling, broken by bluffs covered with pines. At a pass flanked on each side with timbered bluffs, the hunters had caught up with the rear of a moving mass of buffalo. The men killed some buffalo, prepared the meat by cutting it in strips and letting it dry in the sun, and returned. This place is now believed to be in the area of St. Paul, Minnesota.

Soon after this report, the entire tribe packed up and headed west. The reason for this initial migration was, of course, a severe drought that drove the game westward and perhaps discouraged what agricultural efforts they had been making at the time. As the story goes, this tribe caught up with the buffalo herds and resumed a more leisurely way of life, maybe even settling down as part-time farmers and part-time hunters in what is now perhaps northern Minnesota and southern Manitoba.

Up to this point, our story is legendary. But here the oral history takes root, as tribal historians pick up the telling of the migration story. In 1932, Cold Wind, then more than ninety years of age, related to me the start of the second phase of the migration of this ancestral tribe. Cold Wind said that, as a young man, he had gone to visit his Hidatsa relatives in North Dakota. From there, he went east and traveled many, many days and finally came to some Indians (probably Indians on the White Earth, Red Lake, or Leech Lake reservations of northern Minnesota). There, he met an old, old man, a tribal historian, who knew stories about the ancestors of the Hidatsa. This old man took Cold Wind on a trip farther east and north for the purpose of showing him the abandoned village of the ancestral tribe. They came to a valley, and along the river were the caved-in sites of the earthen lodges and other structures of a village. Next, the old man took Cold Wind up on a nearby bench and showed him tepee rings. Then he said to Cold Wind, "According to our historians, your ancient ones, the forefathers of your people, once lived here. These tepee rings were used by a part of the tribe who preferred to live in tepees during the summer and hunt the buffalo, while the others lived in the village along the river and did some farming. Then, one day the two groups got together and moved away. They headed southwestward and never came back!"

As Cold Wind continued the story into what we may regard as Episode II of this migration narrative, he became more positive and explicit; he mentioned names of persons and of places. His informants and teachers were the octogenarians, and older, of his youthful years. It was about 1550 A.D. that this ancestral tribe deliberately moved away southwestward, either looking for better hunting and farming grounds or fleeing from hostile tribes from the east. In all probability, a combination of these circumstances contributed to this phase of the unusual tribal migration. We now know that, as eastern tribes acquired firearms from European traders, the bow-and-arrow Indians were pushed farther and farther west. Nearly all of the present Montana tribes migrated there from the eastern woodlands.

Cold Wind continued that, on the way, these migrants stopped for some time at Sacred Waters (Devil's Lake in northeastern North Dakota). The Hidatsa have a creation legend identifying this lake as the place where their progenitors emerged from a cave after a long subterranean trip from the southeast. But the Crow historians tell a real story: Here on the shores of this lake, two chiefs—No Vitals and Red Scout—fasted and sought the Great Spirit's guidance on their perilous journey. Red Scout received an ear of corn and was told to settle down and plant the seeds for his sustenance. No Vitals received a pod of seeds and was told to go west to the high mountains and plant the seeds there. These seeds were sacred, and the proper way to use them would be revealed to the people when they got there someday. The Great Spirit promised No Vitals that his people would someday increase in numbers, become powerful and rich, and own a large, good, and beautiful land!

The journey was resumed and by the turn of the seventeenth century, the band had reached the Missouri River and moved in with the Mandans, whose village was located on the west side of the river near the junction of the Heart River with the Missouri. Later, the newcomers moved farther upstream and built their own village of earthen lodges in the vicinity of the confluence of the Knife River and the Missouri River.

It was probably between 1600 and 1625 A.D. that No Vitals, now middle-age, finally decided to go westward to plant the sacred seeds and look for the promised land. Using a women's quarrel over meat as an excuse, No Vitals announced that as soon as spring came he planned to move away. It is said that he announced, "It is time I heed the Great Spirit's instruction. I have tarried too long. Those who want to go with me are welcomed."

Thus, one spring morning there was hurried activity in the village. Large dogs and tamed wolves were harnessed to travois. As relatives bade farewell, No Vitals and about four hundred tribe members faced westward and left. Thus began perhaps one of the longest and most dramatic migrations of any Indian tribe, covering thousands of miles over rough and rugged terrain, through intense winters and torrid summers, and consisting of about one hundred years of wandering.

It has been assumed by white historians and archaeologists that this secessionist tribe straightaway entered present Montana, either by following the Missouri all the way up to the three forks or by going up the Yellowstone and then "disappearing" for a long period of time. According to accepted Crow oral history, however, this was not the case. Contemporary tribal historians relate in detail how No Vitals's band traveled up the Missouri and settled in the Cardston, Alberta, area for quite some time. The band probably trekked up the White Bear River (Milk River) in a northwesterly direction.

The ethnohistorical concept that the incipient tribe traveled very slowly as it gradually experienced a cultural transition from sedentary to nomadic lifeways was probably not the case. When No Vitals left, he started out afresh as a brand-new tribe without a name; he literally and symbolically decided to travel light, for he left all the heavy impedimenta behind him for good. His band became an instant tribe capable of existing as a separate and distinct entity, and one motivated with the desire and dream of someday receiving the blessings of the Great Spirit when it reached the promised land!

Episode III of our story started in the Cardston country. The people of this new tribe, still without a name, referred to themselves as "Our Side." One day, the leaders called a council. The consensus of opinion was: "This place is too harsh; the winters are long and cold. We must move and find a better place to live." Once again, they packed their dogs and wolves and headed south through the valleys and passes of the Rocky Mountains. Just how many moons or winters the wandering tribe traveled through was never specifically mentioned.

Then, one day, the wanderers came out of the mountains onto a large plateau. They came to a lake that was described as "so large that the other side could not be seen" and so salty that they could not drink it. There is no question but that this was the Great Salt Lake of the present state of Utah. It is not known how long this tribe stayed here, but they apparently disliked the arid land and decided to move on once again. This time they headed eastward.

The details of this eastward trek are lacking until the band came to an impressive landmark. It was a huge pit in the ground with a roaring fire at the bottom. They called this place "Where There Is a Fire." It was apparently a burning coal vein at the time, but must have caved in long ago. It may have been located somewhere in the present states of Wyoming, Colorado, northern New Mexico, or northern

Texas. From this Place of Fire, our story fades into the legendary once again. Only fragmentary mention of certain places and things indicates that the migrant tribe continued its eastward trek. One version of the story indicates that, as they continued on, they finally came to a large river flowing to the east. As they followed this river downstream, they found many arrowheads and other stone artifacts along the banks. They called this river "Arrowhead River," now identified as the Canadian River of north Texas and Oklahoma. The group continued and eventually came to a forest country. Here, they noticed flocks of large birds with striped wing and tail feathers (turkeys). The people didn't like this place since "they could not see distant places" because of the trees. This was probably in the present states of Oklahoma and Arkansas or even Missouri.

Once again, the decision was made to turn and go in another direction. This time, the group headed north and west. Just how it emerged once more onto the prairie country of the Western Plains is not known. The tribal historians are mute about this segment of the migration. It may be conjectured that the migrants either followed the Arkansas River or the Missouri River upstream. If they followed the latter river, they could have turned directly westward by going up the Platte River and eventually entering into what is now northern Wyoming and southern Montana, the very region they called their own land in the 1851 Fort Laramie Treaty. This Platte River excursion is feasible since neither Crow historians nor those of other tribes along the Missouri have any records of a group coming up the Missouri in recent times, say toward the end of the eighteenth century.

When the wandering tribe finally arrived in this area of present southern Montana and northern Wyoming, the people were still pedestrians. No Vitals, who led the exodus around the turn of the seventeenth century, had been succeeded as head chief by his protégé, Running Coyote. He was entrusted with the care of the sacred seeds given to Chief No Vitals at the Sacred Waters. This same chief was also credited with originating the Crow technique of stampeding buffalo over cliffs.

Succeeding head chiefs—called the "chiefs before the coming of the horse and the white man"—were listed as Paints His Body Red, Red Fish, One Heart, Raven Face, and White Moccasin Top. It appears that, by the time the tribe was already there, One Heart was the head chief. He often succeeded in entrapping buffalo on slick ice around ice holes in the Yellowstone River where the buffalo would come to drink. Many animals could be killed in this manner.

Chief Young White Buffalo, who succeeded White Moccasin Top as head chief, was regarded as being instrumental in transforming the new tribe from walking to horseback-riding Indians about 1734 or 1735. His war parties brought back horses from the south about this time. Also, while he was chief, the tribe first obtained steel knives from the northern tribes, who acquired them from the French traders in Canada.

Crow oral history from the time of One Heart and Raven Face, who were contemporaries, to the present is well recorded.

In closing, may I again take courage to state that when No Vitals led the exodus of some four hundred people away from the ancestral village along the Missouri, the break was made quickly and cleanly. The new tribe left its material culture behind; there was no gradual transition from the earth lodge to the tepee!

The migration was purposely made. It was motivated by the dream of one man named No Vitals. At the Sacred

Waters, the Great Spirit promised him a good land far to the west where his people would find the good life one day. Yes, it took about one hundred years of wandering through the wilderness over long, long distances. The original migrants all died along the way, but it was their great-great-grandchildren and their children who brought the sacred seeds to the great mountains of the west—the Beartooths, the Crazy Mountains, the Bighorns, the Wind River Mountains, the Absarokas, and even the Grand Tetons.

Indeed, this is the land the great Crow chief Arapooish described as "a good country because the Great Spirit had put it in exactly the right place."

Esak
Ebandia

Plays With His Face

About the time the colonists won their independence and became a new nation, tribes of the Western Plains lived by the hunt for their subsistence and conducted intertribal warfare for their avocation. Their life was a continuous drama, a drama that only Mother Earth can produce. Each day was a new episode offering new lands, new challenges, and new experiences. One day they picked berries, the next day they hunted the buffalo, on another day they met the enemy tribe on the battlefield—and that night they enjoyed the victory dance, where recognition and honor were given to the young warriors who had fought courageously. Yes, to these nomads of the Plains, bravery was the highest of the desired qualities: It was the standard by which young men gained social prestige; it was through performing brave war deeds that a man attained chieftaincy.

There lived among the Absarokee in that time a very brave man whose deeds were unparalleled to this day. He was called Plays With His Face. He was greatly respected and feared by his fellow tribesmen, but he never acknowledged it. Being a man of quiet and gentle disposition, he showed no outward signs of violence, but when forced, compelled, and challenged, he was no ordinary man to deal with. His creed was to do the impossible and to succeed when others failed. He defied the prowess of men, scorned the dangers of animals, and challenged the powerful forces of nature. He ridiculed death itself!

The Absarokee were proud that among them was the bravest of all brave men. The enemy tribes of the Absarokee, however, held a different view of this man; they greatly respected his bravery on the battlefield and feared his pugnacity. Sioux mothers would merely mention his name to make their children behave.

The story goes that when Plays With His Face was a small lad he tagged along with some older boys on a rabbit hunt. During the chase the little one was left behind and was lost. Men of the tribe hunted for him for several days and gave him up as devoured by wolves or bears. Then suddenly the boy returned to camp by no means tired or hungry from his ordeal. The wise ones of the tribe soon surrounded the boy and wondered how such a small child could manage to stay alive and return not at all hungry or fatigued. Medicine men then asked him about his experience. He innocently said that "someone" whom he could not see took care of him. This was sufficient. The medicine men nodded at one another and closed the council. All agreed that one of the Great Spirit's helpers had come to protect and help the boy and had given him supernatural powers. They predicted that someday the lad would become a famous man!

In the ensuing years the youngster grew up as an ordinary boy, occasionally doing an unusual thing or feat. At age eighteen he was recognized as a full-fledged man and given his place in the hunt and on the warpath. New experiences soon nurtured the development of a force within the young man. Before long, men of the tribe, fellow hunters and warriors, became aware of Plays With His Face's unusual cunning and bravery.

One enduring story about Plays With His Face involves his encounter with a grizzly bear, which was indeed a dramatic display of his bravery. After all-day travel the Absarokee stopped to camp for the night. Women were busy putting up the tepees and men were tending their horses when a commotion erupted at the edge of the encampment. Women and children screaming, dogs barking frantically, people running, and guns exploding—the noise would pause only to break forth again. All the excitement was caused by a grizzly bear protecting her cubs in a thicket. "She's in that brush behind the big tree," cautioned a bystander as some men armed with guns as well as bows and arrows approached. Then the bear charged again, but the bullets could not stop the big beast and the men fled in all directions. With collected courage they came back, only to be quickly repulsed by the wounded, now enraged bear.

About this time a group of young men came strolling through the camp, including Plays With His Face. When they noticed armed men running around, they hastened toward a group talking excitedly. Some wanted to make another charge, and some even wanted to move camp immediately.

Without saying a word, Plays With His Face walked toward the bear's lair holding a large knife. He stopped and came back. He then took a rope and tied one end around his waist, remarking, "In case I am tempted to retreat and run when the bear comes, this rope will hold me." As he approached the lair closer and closer, the chattering of the people ceased to a hushed silence. All eyes were on him. Step by step he came nearer and nearer; still no charge! He reached the nearby tree and quickly tied the other end of the rope around it. Then he hollered and instantly the bear charged with a roar, fangs flashing and huge claws ripping the ground!

Did Plays With His Face run? No—he too was charging! When the rope yanked him back, the grizzly swerved around the man and again scattered the onlookers. As the bear came back toward its brush, there was Plays With His Face waiting. Again the rope prevented him from catching the bear.

After this the bear refused to come out, which is when Plays With His Face untied the rope and chased the bear and her cubs away!

While already he had discredited the grizzly's reputation as the most fearless and ferocious beast, on another occasion this man proved he had no fear of *any* of Mother Earth's dangerous and wicked animals.

This story is about a rattlesnake. As Plays With His Face and some friends were riding around, they suddenly came upon an unusually large rattlesnake. Coiled to strike, the ugly serpent had its head cocked back and was rattling defiantly! "Next to the grizzly, this is the meanest of the Great Spirit's creatures," remarked someone. Another said, "I wonder what would happen if a man gets too close to this thing."

At this, Plays With His Face prodded his horse near the rattler and thrust himself toward it. But before he could touch the snake, it quickly crawled into its hole and escaped. Plays With His Face, rising and walking toward his horse, merely said, "There is your answer."

There were other unusual things that Plays With His Face did. His younger brother, nicknamed Faces Opposite Direction, was almost as accomplished. He duplicated many of his older brother's feats. He too was invulnerable to enemy bullets and arrows. Their deaths however came in an unexpected way.

They were old men when smallpox, the white man's dreaded disease, struck them and many of the Crow people. The older brother whispered to the younger, "My throat is about to close, but I am not going to let the white man's cursed sickness kill me. I am going to kill myself with my gun." The younger brother whispered back and said, "As usual, I will follow you."

But that is another story, which I will tell later.

Bachay
Balat-Chia

~~~~~~~~~~~~~~~~

The Wise Man

The Absarokee, called Crows by the white men, were probably the first of the eastern woodlands Indians to migrate onto the Northern Plains. This took place around the year 1600, but the tribe traveled around extensively, probably for about another hundred years, before settling in the headwaters of the Yellowstone River and the Missouri River in what is now the state of Montana.

From this small tribe came many great men with unusual talents and strange powers. In the mid-nineteenth century there lived a Crow Indian by the name of The Wise Man. He was highly intelligent and could easily control and manipulate humans and animals.

May I tell you about the time he outwitted a grizzly bear and killed him easily with one thrust of his knife? The Wise

Man and a companion were strolling along an animal pathway when they saw a huge grizzly approaching them. The bear's head was down, indicating he was looking for rodents and insects; occasionally he would flip over a slab of rock while looking for ants to lick up.

The companion whispered, "Let us get away before this mean one sees us and charges." The Wise Man replied that this animal was mean but stupid. He cautioned his partner to hide and watch him.

As the mean one was approaching a knoll, The Wise Man quickly shed his clothes and lay prone along the path. In his right hand was a large sharp knife. The bear didn't see the body until he came directly upon it. Instantly he jumped back and stood on his hind legs. He growled, ready to fight. When there was no movement, the grizzly cautiously approached. Still there was no movement. With a huge paw the grizzly whacked The Wise Man across the chest. Next he rolled him over. The bear sniffed the body and apparently decided to bury it to let it spoil for a while before coming back to feast upon it. It is said that bears often do this.

The bear then turned his back toward the "dead man" and started pawing dirt upon it. He stopped, looked over the body, and turned again to continue throwing dirt. Now The Wise Man quickly but quietly rose and crept up to the bear and plunged his huge knife blade into the bear's armpit and ripped his heart. The mean one lurched forward with a loud groan and collapsed. Then his breathing stopped, forever!

On another day, some men were arguing about the most cautious and wary animal. Some said that the coyote was the most intelligent; he will be around when men have killed off all other animals. Other animals such as the weasel, the mountain goat, and the magpie were also mentioned.

Finally one man said, "Yes, such animals are clever and difficult to capture or kill. But," he added, "the wisest and most difficult to catch are the birds. Of all the birds, the sand crane is so wary that no man has ever captured one alive, and no man ever will. Hunters cannot even get close enough to shoot it with a gun or with an arrow." There was the silence that meant agreement.

At this point The Wise Man interrupted and said, "I am ready to bet everything that I own that I can catch a sand crane alive!" Immediately his challenge was answered with matching bets—a horse for a horse, a gun for a gun, and other similar wagers. The Wise Man informed the men that within a few days he would deliver a live crane.

Soon The Wise Man disappeared into the wilderness. It so happened that he knew the location of a prairie swamp where sand cranes nested in the spring. He sneaked as close as he could and watched the routine movements of the birds—when they go out to find food, how long they are gone, and their other activities. He waited until the mother birds left their nests to find food for their chicks. The Wise Man took his clothes off and crawled into the swamp. He took a position near several nests where the chicks were sitting. As he noticed the mother birds coming back, he submerged himself in the water with a hollow reed in his mouth to breathe through.

The returning cranes were indeed wary. They flew around for some time before cautiously landing near their respective nests. When all was calm, The Wise Man emitted a feeble chick call. One crane, apparently thinking that one of her young ones had strayed off, started walking around on long legs. Finally, it came close to the hiding man in the water. Here The Wise Man quickly grabbed the bird by the legs and brought the bird to shore. He tied the thrashing bird with a thong and returned to camp.

He straightaway went around the camp and collected his winnings, which consisted of good weapons, robes, and several horses.

Later I will tell about the time he outwitted a large party of enemy warriors single-handedly. Also there is an interesting account of how The Wise Man arranged to find a good wife for his young son.

Sits in the Middle
of the Land

~~~~~~~~~~~~~~~~

Called Blackfoot by the Whites

S its in the Middle of the Land was born about 1795 and died in the fall of 1877. The white trappers, traders, and government officials called him Blackfoot. At the Fort Laramie treaty of 1868, his mark (**X**) was designated as "Kam-Ne-But-Sa, Blackfoot."

In his biographical sketches of Crow chieftains (*North American Indians*, 1909), Edward S. Curtis wrote:

He came into big time chieftaincy after Red Bear and Twines His Tail died. He was known mainly as a peace chief and dealt wisely with the United States and gained many advantages for his people. He represented the Crow Tribe at the Fort Laramie Treaty negotiations of 1868 and succeeded in having established a 38-million-acre country for his people. While camping near present Cody, Wyoming, in 1877, he and his Sioux wife (also, he had a Crow wife at the same time) died suddenly of pneumonia and were buried in a common cave grave.

His medicine was the white goose. He would wear the head and tail of a goose on his head with two narrow pieces of red flannel streaming back from his headdress. Two broad strips of flannel, with many scalps attached to them, passed around his neck and down his back, like a reverse stole.

Bureau of Indian Affairs records at Crow Agency list Blackfoot's relatives as follows:

Mother—Strikes Plenty Men or Kills Plenty
Brother—Busy Wolf No. 1
Daughter—Two Buffaloes
Sons—Big Snake, Goes Well-known, and Cuts a Hole in It

Also there are indications that he had other children, as he was married to at least four different women. Runs Through the Camp may have been another son, and perhaps he had, by his Sioux wife, a daughter or stepdaughter called Five.

It is said that Blackfoot was a member of the Sorelips clan. Little is known of his career as a warrior or of his ascendancy to the rank of Crow chief. About 1840, a fierce battle known as "Where [our] Warriors Were Chased Back Into Camp" took place at what is now Wyola, Montana. Here Blackfoot, in hand-to-hand combat with a Sioux warrior, subdued him and wrestled his weapon away from him. Thus he counted two war deeds simultaneously. Later, he earned additional war deeds when he led a Crow war party in pursuit of Piegans fleeing north with many Crow horses, including all of Blackfoot's horses. He overtook the Piegans near the Snowy Mountains (the present Lewistown area). In the ensuing battle, he killed and counted coup on two Piegans and captured many horses besides recovering his own. It was often said that these two experiences vaulted Blackfoot into chieftaincy according to the traditions of Crow Indian warfare.

Sits in the Middle of the Land was a contemporary of such Crow chiefs as Iron Bull (White Temple), Flat Belly, Old Dog, Medicine Crow, and Bear Wolf. In 1904 Crow historians told Curtis that after the deaths of Chief Red Bear of the Mountain Crows in 1862 and Chief Twines His Tail of the River Crows in 1867, Blackfoot became the recognized head chief of the entire Crow tribe.

He personally led a delegation of lesser Crow chiefs such as White Swan, Shot in the Jaw, Poor Elk, Wolf Bow, and others to the Fort Laramie treaty council of 1868. His interpreter was Pierre Chienne, a Frenchman raised by the Crows. The treaty contained two provisions that proved especially important in later years: the right of Crows to continue hunting in unoccupied areas adjoining the reservation and the requirement that the government obtain majority consent of the Crow males in council in any future land deals. Blackfoot's foresight in insisting on these provisions has served and protected the Crows well to this day. Until his death in 1877 at the age of about eighty-two, Sits in the Middle of the Land was a wise and able negotiator with the U.S. government and with white people in general.

In W. C. Vanderwerth's *Indian Oratory* (University of Oklahoma Press, 1971), the author described Blackfoot as a "fine physical specimen . . . noted for his long harangues and his eloquence when in treaty and council meetings."

At a council meeting with government officials on August 11–12, 1873, near the present site of Livingston, Montana (Felix R. Brunot presiding), Chief Blackfoot was quoted as saying in part:

I am going to have a long talk with you. My Great Father sent our friends to see us. We see each other; that is good. The Great Spirit made these mountains and rivers for us and all this land. On the other side of the river below [the Yellowstone], there are plenty of buffalo; on the mountains are plenty of elk and black-tailed deer; and white-tailed deer are plenty at the foot of the mountains. All the streams are full of beaver. In the Yellowstone River the whites catch trout; there are plenty of them.

When we set up our lodge poles, one reaches to the Yellowstone; the other on White River [Milk River]; another one goes to Wind River; the other lodges on the Bridger Mountains. This is our land, and so we told the commissioners at Fort Laramie. The commissioners told us at Laramie if we remained good friends of the whites we would be taken care of for forty years. Since we made that treaty it is only five years. You are in a hurry to quit giving us food.

Those mountains are full of mines. The whites think we don't know about the mines, but we do. It is a rich country; the whites are on it; they are stealing our quartz; it is ours, but we say nothing to them. The whites steal a great deal of our money. We do not want them to go into our country.

We will sell the part of our reservation containing the

mountains from Clark's Fork, below the mountains, and the valleys we will not sell. The Crow young men will go to Washington and fix it up, and come back and tell us about it. We will sell you a big country, all the mountains. Now tell us what you are going to give for our mountains? We want plenty for them. Am I talking right?

Plain Feather, the last tribal historian for the Crow Indians, was regarded as the most reliable of all storytellers, with a remarkable memory for details. Before he died, in 1970 at the age of one hundred, I interviewed him about the death of Sits in the Middle of the Land. His account is as follows:

About one year after the big battle on the Little Bighorn [1876], a small band of Crows went hunting from the Yellowstone to the Stinking River [Shoshone River] in what is now the state of Wyoming.

I recall that I was then seven years of age. To this day I remember all the details of that trip. The band reached the Stinking River a short distance below where the city of Cody now is located. The next morning the head men held a short council. Here Chief Sits in the Middle announced that he was going south to a valley where there were still some buffalo left. The other group decided to follow up the Stinking River to the big mountains where there were plenty of deer and bighorn sheep.

My family was with this latter group. That evening we made camp at the forks of the river just above the narrow canyon where a dam is now located. We stayed there that day. Towards evening we sighted two horseback riders galloping in our direction. They were messengers from the other group. They announced that the great chief and his wife suddenly became ill and soon died. They said we were to hasten over there. It is believed that they died of pneumonia.

Immediately tepees came down and we were soon on our way. We arrived early the next morning, just in time for the burial. The bodies, strapped in robes, were taken to the rimrocks of the valley and put into a ledge and then covered up with slabs of rocks. The burial mourning followed, with men and women wailing. They recounted the many great things that the chief did for his people for many years. At that time he was the Chief of All Chiefs, reigning over the two main bands of the Crow Nation. The hunting expedition was called off and we returned to the Yellowstone.

When white settlers came to the valley where Sits in the Middle of the Land was buried, they called the river there Meeteetsie, which is a rough pronunciation of the Crow word *Bachay-chay*, meaning "a good man" or chief. The town of Meeteetsie, Wyoming, is located not far from the burial site. Whenever Crow Indians went to Cody, they would usually go visit the grave site as a sacred shrine.

In the late 1960s a rather mystical thing happened. A clairvoyant woman in Virginia informed Crow leaders that the spirit of a Crow chief had been coming to her. He wanted his remains returned to the Crow people. A delegation of elders led by a spiritual leader journeyed to the Meeteetsie River to search for the burial site of the great chief Sits in the Middle of the Land. After several days of searching, they found a human skeleton wedged beneath an overhanging ledge. The description of the place conformed with the site where Crow elders would visit.

The skeletal remains were carefully packed and brought back to Crow Agency, Montana. The reburial took place on the campus of the Bureau of Indian Affairs. An impressive burial ceremony was held. Today a monument marks the grave of a great Crow Indian chief.

Medicine Crow

Plains Indian warfare, as practiced in those days, was probably the finest sport ever known in this world. No man who loves horseflesh and the bright face of danger but must long to have shared its thrilling chances. It had all the dash and speed of polo, the informality of a fox hunt, the sporting chance of sudden wealth afforded by the modern horse race, and danger enough to satisfy the most reckless. And it was no game for weaklings, for the Plains Indian seldom gave, and never expected, quarter.

Yet its prime object was not bloodshed or manslaughter. . . . [The Indian] fought not so much to damage his enemy as to distinguish himself. . . . Touching or striking the enemy—alive or dead—was the goal of every warrior. It is known as the *coup*, a term borrowed from the French frontiersmen. As a war honor, it ranked far above the mere killing of an enemy. Rescues, wounds, and captured horses or weapons also counted for honors: but the coup was the great prize. And so it was the object of every man to win as many coups as possible, for all social privileges and perquisites depended on this achievement.

Thus does Stanley Vestal, biographer of Sitting Bull, who understood the Indian well, describe the code of the Western Plains before the coming of the white man. Thus did Medicine Crow, the Absarokee, live.

Medicine Crow was a warrior from the time he first went on the warpath at the age of fifteen until his last battle in 1877. He attained chieftaincy about 1870 at the age of twenty-two, and from then on he set the pace for aspiring young warriors of his people. Until his death in 1920, at the age of seventy-two, he was a "reservation chief," concerned with helping the Crow tribe "learn to live in the ways of the white man" as soon and as efficiently as possible. He went to see the Great Father in Washington many times on behalf of his people.

Medicine Crow, whose name is more accurately translated as Sacred Raven, was born somewhere in the Musselshell country in 1848. His father, also a great chief, was Jointed Together, and his mother was One Buffalo Calf. This was a time of trial for the Absarokee, for the population of the tribe had been reduced from more than eight thousand to fewer than one thousand by the smallpox epidemic of the mid-1840s.

Now the tribe had to be made strong again, lest surrounding hostile tribes succeed in finishing the job the deadly pox had begun—annihilating the Crows. Boys had to become men quickly. The youth of the Absarokee accepted the challenge. Some died on the warpath, but those who survived, the boyhood friends of Medicine Crow, became great warriors and wise chieftains. Among these were Plenty Coups and Two Leggings, well known to the white man, and others such as Two Belly, Pretty Eagle, Old Crow, Bellrock, and many more.

Medicine Crow lived his first fifteen years much as his father and forefathers had. As a small boy, he heard the children's tales. Then came the recitals of warriors' deeds. He was trained to run, swim, wrestle, hunt, and ride. He learned the secrets of nature. Last of all he was taught to be a warrior, and his highest ambition was as that of his young friends—he dreamed of becoming first a warrior and then, perhaps, a chief.

Before that could happen, though, by the customs and religion of his people, he had to fast, seek a vision, and find his "medicine," those spirit helpers who protected and aided the fighting men of the Plains. It is believed that Medicine Crow sought his dream at least three times. His first fasting was a severe test, for he chose a high peak in the Crazy Mountains—rocky pinnacles often called the Mean Mountains by the Indians because of their fierce winds and treacherous storms.

Not satisfied, it is recorded in the spoken annals of the Crow people, he sought another dream in the Pryor Mountains in company with another youth (either Two Leggings or Plenty Coups) on the sacred tribal fasting grounds overlooking the canyon of the Bighorn. The places of the third and any subsequent fasts have been clouded by time.

Throughout his life, Medicine Crow seemed able to see into the future, often into the very distant future. It was because of his dreams, and the fact that his people saw his seemingly impossible visions come to pass, that he was revered as a visionary medicine man. (He did not attempt to heal wounds or sickness.)

On one occasion, the young seeker "saw" something black with round legs puffing smoke and pulling boxlike objects behind it coming down the Valley of Chieftains (the Little Bighorn River). Some thirty years later, in 1895, the Big Horn Southern Railroad was completed.

In another vision, a white man came up from the east and said, "I come from the land of the rising sun, where many, many white men live. They are coming and will in time take possession of your land. At that time you will be a great chief of your tribe. Do not oppose these but deal with them wisely and all will turn out all right."

A third vision revealed to Medicine Crow his future home. He saw a white-man's type of house with a large corral nearby, situated on the top of a hill overlooking the junction of the Little Bighorn River and Lodge Grass Creek. About 1910 he built this house where he "saw" it so many years before.

Another vision that became a reality was his dream of the Crow country covered with large herds of the white-man's "horse buffalo"—cattle.

It was during his dreams that Medicine Crow gained his spirit helpers, the eagle and the large hawk that the Absarokee called the "Striped Tail."

As a youth of fifteen, against his mother's wishes but with the help of his stepfather, a war chief, Medicine Crow went on his first war party. He earned no honors but gained valuable experience. In the next nineteen years, until he reached the age of thirty-four, he led the vigorous and often dangerous life of a Plains Indian warrior. For twelve of those years he was a war chief. He was noted for his agility in hand-to-hand combat, his courage, and his dependability as a war party commander who usually brought his men back home not only safely but victoriously.

He was still a young man when he completed the Crow military requirements for attaining chieftaincy. All involved risking one's life. These tests were as follows:

1. To touch or strike the first enemy fallen, whether alive or dead. This was called "counting coup."

2. To wrestle a weapon away from an enemy warrior.

3. To enter an enemy camp at night and steal a horse. Prized war or hunting horses were usually tied to the door of a tepee, or even to the wrist of the owner sleeping inside. This feat was called "cutting the halter rope."

4. To command a war party successfully. The warrior was given this command only after completing the other three requirements. If he brought his party back safely and victoriously, he earned a war deed.

Medicine Crow's exploits are still spoken of by the old men of the Absarokee. He earned the right to be a chief many times over. Some of his most famous deeds were recorded in hieroglyphics before his death by his friend Bird Far Away. The record, on a strip of white cloth three feet wide and twenty-five feet long, is one of my most prized possessions. Space does not permit the retelling of all of the twenty-two war deeds of Chief Medicine Crow, but a few have been selected.

Shortly after his first venture against the Shoshoni, Medicine Crow and three other young warriors went on the warpath during the winter. They traveled through the Pryors to the present site of Cody, Wyoming, and captured four horses belonging to the Shoshoni. The horses were given to relatives, as was the custom. This was Medicine Crow's first war honor.

When Crows and Sioux met in battle near what is now Hardin, Montana, a Sioux warrior was knocked off his horse as two Crows rode by, striking the first and second coups. Medicine Crow grappled with the Sioux and wrestled his rifle away from him, thus earning an honor for taking an enemy's weapon.

Medicine Crow commanded his first war party against the Sioux, who were encamped near the present site of Forsyth, Montana. He sent his warriors into the enemy's camp to capture horses but was not satisfied with their work, so he went in himself and "cut the halter rope" of a prized horse tied to the doorway poles of a tepee. The Absarokee went home with two fine buffalo and war horses, plus a mule, which was regarded as more valuable than a horse.

About 1874 the Crows annihilated seven Sioux warriors on the headwaters of Tullock Creek, east of the present town of Crow Agency. The Sioux entrenched themselves in a deep washout and committed themselves to selling their lives dearly. Several Absarokee had already been killed when Medicine Crow arrived on the scene. Without hesitating, he trotted forward through Sioux fire, jumping from side to side as he ran, and leaped into the nest of desperate enemies. The impact panicked the Sioux, and as they scattered to flee, the Absarokee quickly dispatched them. Though Medicine Crow received only two war honors, one for counting first coup and one for taking an enemy's weapon, some students of Absarokee warfare believe he was truly entitled to seven first coups and two scores for the two rifles he wrestled away from enemies.

Medicine Crow was involved with the United States Army in two major battles with Indians. He was the leader of the 176 Crow warriors who accompanied General Crook at the battle of Rosebud a week before the famed battle at the Little Bighorn on June 25, 1876. Lt. John C. Bourke, in his book *On the Border with Crook*, wrote that the Crows "are somewhat fairer than the other Indians about them. They are all above medium height, not a few being quite tall and many have noble expression of countenance. . . . Medicine Crow, the Crow Chief, looked like a devil in his war bonnet of feathers, furs, and buffalo horns." The Crows did well that day. Only two men were wounded, and none were killed.

Crows were camped along Pryor Creek a short distance north of the gap when a party of Arapaho warriors was discovered nearby. Immediately the chase was on, as the enemy party headed for the gap. Medicine Crow, riding a fast horse, caught up with two fleeing enemy warriors, rode between them, and struck coup on both. At this moment his horse was shot, and as it stumbled forward, Medicine Crow grabbed the Arapaho warriors. The three came tumbling down together. Medicine Crow wrestled a rifle away from one, while the other was quickly dispatched by other Crow warriors. Medicine Crow's war song recited this feat.

On another occasion, Absarokee and Sioux met in a battle at the bend of Pass Creek south of Wyola, Montana. One Sioux warrior made "strong medicine" and raised havoc with the Crows. He seemed invulnerable to bullets and arrows. Medicine Crow called on his sacred helper, the eagle, made strong medicine of his own, and ceremoniously prepared his muzzle-loader. He then approached the taunting Sioux, shot him from his horse, struck first coup, took his weapon, and scalped him by way of defying the Sioux war party (with the Crows, taking scalp was not a war deed).

Again, in 1877, Medicine Crow joined forces with the

United States Army. This time he rode with General Miles against the Nez Perce. One Nez Perce warrior, weary of fighting all the way from Idaho, made signs to the Crows and invited them to count coup on him. Medicine Crow and another Crow immediately accepted the invitation and charged the Nez Perce at full gallop. The Nez Perce fired and killed both of their horses with a single shot. Medicine Crow continued his charge on foot. The Nez Perce quickly reloaded his 45.70 and took aim. Medicine Crow recalled that as he approached, jumping from side to side, he could look right into the huge barrel of the rifle. There was a flash; a bullet tore under Medicine Crow's arm and knocked off his powder horn. Medicine Crow pounced on the desperate Nez Perce, wrestled the rifle away, and then gently allowed him to rejoin his comrades in their futile flight.

Medicine Crow saw the nomadic life of the Plains change to the confinement of the reservation. In the fading winters of his life, he was beginning to discern the ultimate meaning of his boyhood vision: "If you deal wisely with these White Eyes, all will turn out all right and good for your people."

Medicine Crow, the Absarokee chief, went to the happy hunting grounds of his forefathers in July 1920. He was buried on a high hill overlooking the Valley of Chieftains.

A NOTE ON MEDICINE CROW GENEALOGY

Medicine Crow's parents separated while he was a small boy. His mother, One Buffalo Calf, married Sees the Living Bull, a noted medicine man. From this marriage Medicine Crow had one half brother named Little Nest and three half sisters, The Other Beaver, Beaver Place Well-known, and Strikes and Kills Them. The living descendants of these siblings include Mary (Bear All Time) La Forge, Mary (Walks) La Forge, Juanita (Buffalo) Crooked Arm, and the children of the late Edward Big Medicine.

Medicine Crow was married twice and possibly three times. By his second wife (Takes Many Prisoners) he had a daughter named Annie, the mother of the late Mark Real Bird. Mark's descendants today are his children, Edison, Pius, Floyd, Charles, Lorraine, and Margo, and many grandchildren. Chief Medicine Crow's last wife was Medicine Sheep. They had four sons—Cassie, Hugh, Leo, and Chester, all deceased. The descendants of Chester are his children, George, William, and Bertha, and many great-grandchildren. I, Joe Medicine Crow, am the only son of Leo; my children are two daughters, Diane and Vernelle, and one son, Ronald.

Medicine Rock
Chief

~~~~~~~~~~~~~~~~~~~~

A Twentieth-Century Sun Dance Man

T his Crow Indian is enrolled in the records of the Bureau of Indian Affairs as Josiah Thomas Yellowtail. He is now, in January 1992, about eighty-nine years of age.

May I briefly tell you about Mr. Yellowtail's interesting life and about his important decision during middle age to accept the arduous and serious demands of training to become a Sun Dance spiritual leader and his dedication to the Sun Dance Way.

Josiah Thomas Yellowtail was the third and youngest son of Yellowtail and Elizabeth Frazee Chienne. Yellowtail was born about 1855, the son of Rises Upward and Stays by the Water, both full-blood Crow Indians, and as a boy lived in the pre-reservation days before 1870.

Elizabeth Chienne and her younger sister, Mary Chienne

Takes Gun, were so-called mixed bloods, the daughters of Robert Frazee (or Fraser) and Emma Chienne, one of the daughters of Pierre Chienne and his Crow Indian wife, Bear in the Woods. Elizabeth (Lizzie) and Mary were raised by their grandfather, Pierre Chienne, and they used his name when enrolled by the government as one-quarter-degree Crow Indians. Lizzie was born on July 4, 1864, at Fort Benton, Montana Territory, and she died in 1969 at the age of a hundred and five.

The story of Tom Yellowtail's European roots is very interesting. His great-grandfather, Pierre Chienne, was the son of immigrants from France. He came out west up the Missouri River in the early 1800s and became a trader, mountain man, squaw man, and interpreter for the Crow Indians. He married several Indian women, who represented at least three tribes. His first Crow wife was called Kills the Horse Herder; they had many daughters and one son, Frank Chienne. His second Crow wife was Bear in the Woods, the mother of Emma Chienne and thus the grandmother of Tom Yellowtail and his two older, deceased brothers, Carson and Robert, and his two living sisters, Amy Y. Whiteman, age ninety-four, and Agnes Y. Deernose, almost eighty.

A further word about Pierre Chienne. The Crow tribe owes this Frenchman a great deal. He played a very special part in the Fort Laramie treaty of 1868. He was the interpreter for the Crow chief Blackfoot, called Sits in the Middle of the Land by his people. It was stated by Plain Feather, the last great Crow historian, who died in 1970 at the age of one hundred, that Pierre Chienne practically wrote the provisions of the treaty that have served the tribe well to this day. Plain Feather said this man was one white man who spoke the Crow language fluently, without a trace of foreign accent.

Another part of Tom Yellowtail's French background came to him by way of Scotland. An ancestor originally from Normandy crossed the Channel during the conquest of England in the eleventh century. The Norman family of Friselle or Fresel, and later Fraisier, became established in Scotland in the twelfth and thirteenth centuries, rising to political prominence as the chief power in Tweeddale, but when Simon Fraser, the Lord Lovat, was beheaded for his part in the Jacobite Rebellion, the other Fraisers fled to France. Here the family name became Frazee. After the Pretender died, some of the Frazees returned to Scotland, and some of these rose to prominence again. Sir James Fraser, the scholar and author of *The Golden Bough*, the classic study of primitive religion, was one famous member of the family.

Ephraim Frazee, born in Scotland about 1640–45, was the immigrant ancestor of the American Frazees. He founded Elizabethtown, New Jersey. Robert Fraser or Frazee, a grandson, came out west and married Emma Chienne, Pierre Chienne's half-Crow daughter, in early 1860. Elizabeth, Tom Yellowtail's mother, was born about 1864.

And what about the man Tom Yellowtail himself, his physical appearance, his personality, his character, and other inherent attributes? Tom is generally described as "not tall and not short." He was nicknamed the Light One because of his fair complexion and brownish gray eyes. The girls of the tribe considered him very handsome and called him *Ba-baru-Sabish*, an expression equivalent to the popular "super."

Considering his diversified genetic heritage, we would expect Tom Yellowtail to display certain strong and significant ethnic traits and characteristics. This is not the case! Tom can be more accurately described as an average and well-balanced individual. He is regarded as good-natured and easygoing; he is not given to impulsive reactions but is always able to control himself and to resolve problems quite logically. In short, Tom Yellowtail is a good man! He is kind, friendly, understanding, and caring of others. It is a blessing to know him and to be his friend.

I have said that I've known him quite well for many years. I knew him as a student at Lodge Grass High School, where he was the star basketball player. At Bacone College in Oklahoma he played basketball and football and was a shot-putter on the track team. I have seen him ride bucking horses at local rodeos, play baseball as a catcher, and wrestle the reservation middleweight champion.

Tom is generally slow and deliberate in his movements, but when necessary he moves as fast and agilely as a cat. Once on a hunt he sneaked up on a sleeping buck deer and jumped on his back. As the deer sprang up and lurched forward, Tom stayed on top and soon cut the deer's throat. Then there was the time he crawled along the bottom of a deep hole in the Little Bighorn River and grabbed a huge trout by the gills. Tom's wife, Susie, always regarded his catching the wary trout as a "fish story."

On another afternoon, Tom and his five-year-old son were in the field irrigating when a windy storm suddenly hit. As they were hurrying home, a pheasant flushed out and took flight. The boy cried, "Shoot! Shoot!" Tom pointed the shovel toward the flying bird and hollered, "Boom!" And the bird came tumbling down dead. Tom didn't explain to the boy that the bird had hit a telephone line. The boy told his mother that his daddy was a "good shooter." But again Susie was sure Tom was telling another fish story.

Thomas Yellowtail was brought up strictly in the Crow Indian way by his pre-reservation parents. He was a good Crow, because he understood and respected the clan codes of behavior; he participated in Crow Indian doings such as the social and ritual dances, and he was a member of several ceremonial societies.

The Crow Indians use several methods of evaluating a person's status in society. One way is to recognize the number of names a person has. Tom Yellowtail has been given five different names in his lifetime, each time in recognition of a particularly outstanding achievement. His favorite name is still the one given to him soon after his birth by Chief Medicine Crow. The chief selected the name Medicine Rock Chief, commemorative of his ownership of a sacred carved stone to which he attributed his success as a warrior and, later, as one of the greatest war chiefs of the Crow Nation. For the past thirty-eight years Tom Yellowtail has been motivated by his first given name as he serves as a chief in the sacred ways of the Crow people.

And now it is my difficult task to try to analyze and to explain as simply as possible Medicine Rock Chief's dedication to the Crow Sun Dance religion and his thoughts about other areas of native Crow religion and philosophy.

As a young boy, Tom Yellowtail was exposed simultaneously to the sacred Crow ways and to Christianity. When the Yellowtails enrolled two of their children, Carson and Amy, at the new Baptist day school in Lodge Grass, Montana, the Catholic Church excommunicated Yellowtail, a devout Catholic. The family then left the Catholic Church and joined the new Baptist mission.

Tom has been a member of the First Crow Indian Baptist Church at Lodge Grass for the past seventy-five years. He still attends services and other church functions, if not on a regular basis. He does not reject Christian doctrines nor attempt to superimpose Sun Dance ways over them. In fact, this man has admirably blended and synthesized the two systems into an integrated, meaningful, and spiritually comfortable way of life. In his prayers he interchanges the Christain words "God" and "Christ" with the Crow expression "Above Old Man" without conflict of feelings. He understands the meaning of Jesus's fasting forty days as he understands a Sun Dance man's fasting four days in the "big lodge." He understands Jesus's telling his disciples to lay hands on a person for healing as he understands the Sun Dance chief's touching a person with feathers for healing.

The man called Medicine Rock Chief is both self-made and a born holy man in the Sun Dance way of worship. He was self-made because he accepted a challenging training; he was born to be a holy man because he was blessed with the intelligence and innate qualities required of such a man.

Priests, shamanists, and holy men of all races and places come into being when their people are confronted by unusual and overwhelming events that disrupt the ordinary way of living. When all attempts to bring relief fail, then the sad situation is attributed to the gods, to supernatural powers. At this point, the people try in desperation to establish rapport with the supernatural powers in order to regulate them. While this is going on, here steps forward a special person with a solution. He has a good definition of the situation and will, therefore, release the people from their bondage.

This special person is the product of three factors coming into conjunction: First is the event or situation at hand; second is a man with capability and intelligence; and third is this man's definition of the situation, which leads to the solution's becoming a reality. The result of the successful conjunction of these three factors is the emergence of a new leader, who brings about the final release of the people from their predicament.

Medicine Rock Chief was born to be a spiritual leader because of his inherent intelligence and inner qualities. He came forward at a time when his people were impoverished by a decade of drought and economic depression. Furthermore, a terrible war in Europe was taking place; almost daily fine Crow youths were being inducted into the armed forces of the United States, and some were already on the battle fronts of faraway foreign lands.

Certainly the Crow people faced a predicament. At this point, in the late 1930s and early 1940s, Tom Yellowtail embraced the Sun Dance Way, which had been brought recently to the Crow Indian Reservation. In the big lodge he would dance under a tortuous sun hour after hour, offering propitiation prayers to the Above Old Man for the Crow youths in the armed forces, praying for an early end to the war, praying for a lasting peace. He would subject himself to fasting for three days and three nights and endure the tortures of the ritual dances several times during the summer.

While participating in these torrid ritual dances, he was, in fact, training to be a medicine man, that is, a holy man with healing powers and good prayers. He was in the process of being made and perhaps did not realize it until he was noticed by John Trejillo, the great Sun Dance chief of the Shoshoni tribe of Wyoming, Idaho, and Utah and the Crow tribe of Montana. Several Crow Indian Sun Dance aspirants sought the blessings of the aged John Trejillo, known as the Venerable Rainbow. Some boldly asked him to give them power. Competition for the position as his successor was intense, but he would answer that his medicine fathers would tell him when to select the chosen one.

One day it happened. At the conclusion of a dance at Fort Washakie, the Venerable Rainbow called Thomas Yellowtail of the Crow tribe to come to the center pole. Here he formally transferred his leadership position in the Sun Dance to Medicine Rock Chief. He thereupon gave his sacred healing eagle-feather wand to his successor and pronounced his blessing on him. At this moment Thomas Yellowtail was made a Sun Dance medicine man.

In bringing this short biography to a close, I wish to point out that Tom Yellowtail was given a prophetic name, and it took the major portion of his life to achieve the status of a "chief" in the arduous Sun Dance religion. I would also take poetic license to allude to Tom's Scottish heritage by imagining that when dressed up for the dance in his colorful wraparound skirt, he would be the very picture of his ancient Scots ancestors—in the eleventh and twelfth centuries, kilts were long. I may go on to imagine that Tom Yellowtail, a late-twentieth-century religionist, personifies some of the theories set forth by his distant Fraser relative in *The Golden Bough.*

Intertribal Warfare in the Wolf Mountains

~~~~~~~~~~~~~~~~~

THE HILL WHERE A GROS VENTRE WAR PARTY WAS ANNIHILATED (MASSACRE HILL)

In the latter part of the 1860s or early 1870s, prior to the Custer battle of 1876, the Crows discovered a band of Hairy Nostrils (Prairie Gros Ventres) and chased them up a hill in the Wolf Teeth Mountains at the headwaters of the south fork of Rosebud Creek.

The Hairy Nostrils dug in and were soon well fortified. They taunted the Crows to come and get them and made obscene gestures at them. Several Crow warriors who attempted to dislodge them were killed. Crazy Head, a proven warrior and prospective chieftain, charged up to the

The author pointing out the path of Custer's troops at the Little Bighorn. (*Smithsonian Institution*)

The author (center) with longtime friend (and project editor for the Library of the American Indian) Herman Viola (left) in a tepee at the Crow Fair. (*Smithsonian Institution*)

Medicine Crow, grandfather of the author. The high pompadour is typical of Crow men. This photo was taken during a visit to Washington, D.C. (*National Anthropological Archives, Smithsonian Institution*)

Medicine Crow, again, as an older man. (*National Museum of the American Indian, Smithsonian Institution*)

White-Man Runs Him, one of General Custer's six Crow scouts, in traditional battle garb. (*National Museum of the American Indian, Smithsonian Institution*)

CURLY WHITE MAN RUNS HIM HAIRY MOCCASIN

THE THREE SURVIVING CUSTER SCOUTS AT THE 45ᵗʰ ANNIVERSARY OF CUSTER'S BATTLE

AA 11

Of Custer's six Crow scouts, three were still alive to pose for this photograph on the occasion of the forty-fifth anniversary of the Battle of the Little Bighorn. From left to right: Curly, White-Man Runs Him, and Hairy Moccasin. (*National Museum of the American Indian, Smithsonian Institution*)

As described in the foreword, the author was surprised to find this family photograph in the National Anthropological Archives. From left to right: Amy White Man (née Yellowtail, daughter of well-known Crow warrior chief Yellowtail and sister of Robert Yellowtail), her nephew Beauford Yellowtail (son of Robert), Arlis White Man (son of John White Man), and John White Man (one of two sons of White-Man Runs Him). The author is missing from this 1923 photograph because he had chosen not to accompany his family to Washington, D.C. (*National Anthropological Archives, Smithsonian Institution*)

Medicine Crow (right) leading a dance in the Crow country. (*National Museum of the American Indian, Smithsonian Institution*)

Still the Crow country, but many years later, the honor guard leads the Crow Fair parade through the encampment. (*Smithsonian Institution*)

Typical dress of participants in the Crow Fair parade. (*Smithsonian Institution*)

Many tepees dot the landscape in this aerial view of the Crow Fair, which takes place each summer at Crow Agency on the Crow Reservation in southern Montana. (*Smithsonian Institution*)

fortification and was thrusting a coup stick into it when he was shot in the abdomen.

At this point, the Crow chieftains in charge of the operation called a halt and held a conference. What to do with about sixty warriors strongly fortified and entrenched on a high hilltop, that was the question. It was decided to dispatch emissaries to a friendly Sioux band camped in the Rosebud Creek area not far to the east, to invite their warriors to participate in the assault on a common enemy. The Crows had only recently made peace and had become allies with this particular Sioux band. As the emissaries rode off, the enemy on the hill was informed that the Sioux would be coming soon; the Hairy Nostrils could expect a battle for their lives. They retorted with jeers and made insults in sign language.

Before the shadows moved the length of a horse quirt (about an hour), there was commotion on the hill when the Hairy Nostrils saw the approach of the Sioux. Clouds of dust swirled up, gun barrels flashed through the dust, and the rumble of horses' hooves and war whoops became louder and louder as the Sioux horde rapidly advanced. Just as the unfortunate warriors from the north were reinforcing their fortress feverishly, the Sioux struck! The lead riders jumped off their mounts and without hesitation started up the hill under cover of a dense hail of arrows that were being arched into the fort. The Gros Ventres were absolutely powerless to fight back under such an onslaught of arrows. They quickly panicked and rushed out, each man for himself.

As the Gros Ventres ran down the hill in all directions, the Crows moved in and picked them off. About sixty Gros Ventre warriors were killed, few escaped that day. It is said that seven or eight arrived at an appointed place in the Little

Bighorn Valley about three miles north of what is now the town of Lodge Grass and went home. After the intertribal war era, one of these escapees, known as White Shirt, visited the Crows and collaborated with Crow historians in the authentic recounting of this great battle in the Wolf Mountains.

Crooked coup sticks were given to those Crow warriors who took the suicidal oath to die fighting for the people during a period of one year. In the case of this battle, Crazy Head, a foolhardy warrior, had deliberately taken away a crooked stick from its rightful holder to dramatize his bravery. Crazy Head recovered from his wound and became a great Crow chief. Another famed Crow warrior and promising chief, Repulses the Enemy, was less fortunate. When the Gros Ventres tumbled out of their fort and fled down the hill toward the timber, he carelessly came between two fleeing Gros Ventres and was grabbed and stabbed to death.

FOUR CROW WAR PARTIES MOVE INTO THE WOLF MOUNTAINS

By necessity, the Crow were militaristic. Besieged on all sides by enemy tribes, at one time or another, Crow warriors were often on the warpath.

In the late 1860s, four parties of Crow warriors moved simultaneously against the Sioux in the Wolf Mountains area. A party of only two men, Sweet Marrow and a trusted comrade, left the big bend of the Yellowstone (the area of present-day Livingston, Montana) and went toward the Wolf Teeth Mountains by way of the Pryor Mountains and the Bighorn Mountains. Near the mouth of the Tongue River, Sweet Marrow, a reputable medicine man, made ritual. By looking through his pipestem, like a telescope, he "saw" and knew the progress of the other parties.

The main party was originally led by Flathead Woman, a successful Pipe Carrier commander. As Flathead Woman left the Crow camp on the Yellowstone and headed east toward the Wolf Teeth, he was continuously joined by warriors. By the time he camped in the Sioux Pass area, he had accumulated a sizable array of warriors, including several noted Pipe Carriers. This made Pipe Carrier Flathead Woman quite happy and proud that so many had joined him. He was now the leader of many!

Then it happened! The other Pipe Carriers announced their own plans and asked volunteers to join them. Blackbird-on-the-Ground, also a reputable Pipe Carrier, announced that he was heading for a Sioux camp at Cold Springs up Otter Creek. He called for volunteers and many joined him. Another Pipe Man, Wolf Bear, who proclaimed that "seven enemy warriors were given him," headed north with many volunteers.

This sudden turn of events left Flathead Woman with only one warrior, a man named Two Whistles. Flathead Woman was hurt indeed! Nevertheless, the two went on with Two Whistles acting as a scout and traveling some distance ahead. The dejected Pipe Carrier came behind and cried audibly so that his Spirit Protector would have pity on him and give him success on this warpath.

They came to the junction of Indian Creek and Rosebud Creek, where they found a warriors' lodge and stayed for the night. Two Whistles addressed Flathead Woman: "Chief of the Wolves, do not feel sad. I have a feeling that we two will have good luck and go home with good war deeds."

Early the next morning, the Pipe Carrier sent out his "wolf" (scout) to reconnoiter upstream. His instruction to Two Whistles was a riddle: Look for a sidehill spring (of water) where he would find a snake frozen in the spring (season of the year). This would promise success. And it was not long before the scout hastened back and reported just such a find! That night, the two crept into a Sioux camp on the Tongue River and captured about forty head of horses, including a prized dark sorrel. Flathead Woman personally "cut the halter rope." A few days later, these two intrepid warriors returned to the Crow camp victoriously!

In the meantime, Wolf Bear's "wolves" were ranging the headwaters of the "Creek Where Many Colts Died" (Tullock Creek). It was not long before a small Sioux war party was discovered and surrounded. The Sioux jumped into a washout and the siege was on. The Sioux were well concealed and fortified and had already killed several Crows when a promising young warrior named Medicine Crow arrived. Never hesitating, he charged toward the enemy, dodging and weaving as the Sioux opened fire. He jumped right into the washout filled with seven Sioux. They panicked and were scattering out when they were quickly overwhelmed and annihilated. The Sioux lookout concealed on a nearby hill escaped and fled toward the camp at Cold Springs on Otter Creek. On the way, he nearly ran into Crow warriors fleeing westward, apparently from the direction of the Cold Springs Sioux camp.

When this lone Sioux survivor reached his camp the next morning, the people were having a victory (or scalp) dance over the body of a dead Crow. He was Well-Known Magpie, the handsomest man of the Crow tribe, who had been killed during the night raid. The body had not been abused, as was the usual practice of the Sioux. Well-Known Magpie was propped up against a log, and he was indeed handsome, even in death. Sioux women came to admire him, lingered too long, and were beaten by jealous husbands, or so the Sioux later related. But when the returning Sioux warrior reported the annihilation of his seven comrades, the Sioux turned on the body of the handsome Crow and hacked it into pieces.

Now, what had happened to Blackbird-on-the-Ground's excursion to the Sioux camp at Cold Springs? The party had succeeded in capturing horses and were just leaving when Well-Known Magpie went back to "cut the halter rope" on a good horse he saw tied in front of a lodge. He was discovered and fired at in the dark as he fled. The pursuit was continued into the following day. At dusk the Sioux stopped and decided to give up the chase when they heard a Crow singing a praise song somewhere from the northwest. The singing came from Wolf Bear's party, camped at the junction of the Little Bighorn River and Dense Ash Trees Creek, or Reno Creek. The Sioux decided to continue the chase during the night and catch up with the Crows early in the morning.

The strategy worked. Early the next morning, they caught up with the rear guard of the Crows fleeing from the Cold Springs incident. At the first skirmish the horse of Yellow Leggings was shot. The unfortunate Crow warrior fled on foot, but he was overtaken and killed. Soon, another man's horse was killed and he too was at the mercy of the Sioux. With a loaded rifle, he stood his ground as a Sioux riding a dark gray horse charged. At the last second, the rider apparently changed his mind and reined out when his horse slipped on the icy ground and glided to a stop at the waiting Crow's feet. Before the horse could get up, the Crow had mounted him, and they galloped away. Here the Sioux quit and returned. This encounter happened near the summit of the Wolf Mountains between the headwaters of Thompson Creek and a tributary of the south fork of Reno Creek, southeast of the present SU Ranch.

Now back to Sweet Marrow, high up the side of the Big-horn Mountains near Tongue River Canyon where he was "making medicine." After looking through his pipestem, he said to his partner: "I see Flathead Woman driving about forty head of horses toward the Crow camp. I see Blackbird-on-the-Ground fleeing homeward in distress. The yellow feather [Well-Known Magpie's medicine feather] is lying on the ground. I see Wolf Bear heading home singing victory songs."

Sweet Marrow and his companion found a small enemy camp that night where they captured horses and went home victoriously.

THE BATTLE OF PRYOR CREEK

The Dakota, particularly the Hunkpapa and the Oglala, routinely came to the Crow country on horse-capturing and coup-counting raids. Intertribal warfare on the Plains was the dangerous sport through which young men climbed the military ladder to attain chieftaincy. A warrior must complete four acts of bravery to become a chief. This was the essence of Plains Indian warfare, not goals of booty, territory, or conquest.

By the mid-nineteenth century, the surging western expansion of the United States impacted the Sioux and Cheyenne then dwelling in the area now called North and South Dakota. This pressure drove the tribes westward. Their excursions into the Crow country became more frequent and more hostile. The traditional eastern boundary of Crow land was the Powder River, but soon it was replaced by the Tongue River, fifty miles to the west. By 1865 the Sioux and their Cheyenne allies were in the Bighorn Valley, harassing wagon trains on the Bozeman Trail going to the gold fields in the Rocky Mountains.

In fact, by 1860 these tribes began considering occupying the Crow country, which was then still unmolested by the ever more numerous white men.

The story I am now going to tell is about a seriously planned invasion and attempted conquest of the Crows about 1860 or 1861. The site of the great battle of Pryor Creek is only twenty miles south of what is now Billings, Montana.

In 1955 it was my good fortune to have acquired a reliable Sioux version of the battle from Charles Ten Bear, a Crow Indian historian. He explained that about 1910 an old Sioux Indian and his wife came to the Crow Reservation and lived with Yellow Crane, where Charles Ten Bear was also living for the winter. This Sioux man was a survivor of the big battle of Pryor Creek and often would tell the whole story in detail. Furthermore, in 1935 Joe Childs, a fine Crow historian, told me the Crow account of the battle. He said his father, Child in the Mouth, had been an active participant in the conflict and never tired of telling and retelling the battle story. Joe Childs would say, "I've heard the story so many times that I know all about it as if I were there myself." One afternoon this fine storyteller and I sat on a hill overlooking the Pryor Creek battlefield. After smoking tobacco in silence for a while, Joe Childs commenced. But first the Sioux story.

In the early summer of 1859 or 1860, a Crow war party killed a fine young Dakota warrior. Already he had counted a number of battle coups, which entitled him to wear an eagle-feather war bonnet. His mother was overwhelmed with grief and decided to mourn until her son's death was avenged. Almost every evening this distressed mother would lead her son's horse through the camp. The horse, a dark roan, was always bridled, saddled with the late warrior's war bonnet tied to the saddle horn, and ready to go. As she passed the row of tepees, the woman would wail and challenge the warriors. "Is there a man among the mighty Dakotas who will take this horse and go fight the Absarokee? Only when my son's death is avenged will I cease mourning!"

She repeated this performance almost daily for one whole year.

This daily routine was disturbing to the warriors and brought misgivings to the elders, particularly to the medicine men, who concluded that what the woman was doing was not good. Her lament portended misfortune to the tribe. But even the chiefs could not dissuade her from wailing constantly through the camp.

Then one day the situation changed abruptly and dramatically. A young man named Brave Wolf came forward. He had a good reason for this. Brave Wolf was very much in love with a maiden and wanted to make her his woman. According to custom, he asked his sisters and aunts to arrange a wedding. The women were silent. An outspoken aunt finally said they did not like the girl and did not want her as a sister-in-law or daughter-in-law. The young man was deeply hurt and decided to kill himself. In those days a man might commit suicide by killing himself directly with a weapon or by joining the Brave Hearts, the warriors who took the suicidal oath to die fighting for their people. By allowing himself to be killed by an enemy, Brave Wolf would die with glory. Brave Wolf decided to join the Brave Hearts and die fighting the Raven People, as the Dakota sometimes called the Crows.

Brave Wolf had already made up his mind by the time

the wailing woman approached. He arose, walked deliberately, and took the reins of the dark roan war horse. At this moment the woman changed her cry and began a song of victory, emitting the loud Dakota women's shrill. "At last, a brave one has taken my son's horse!" Within moments a big crowd gathered around to see the intrepid young man. Brave Wolf was the instant hero that day!

Quickly a council was called, and to the assembly a leading chief spoke: "This is not just one man's decision; by his action today, we, the Dakota, are committed in what could be a very important and serious undertaking. I ask if the Wakan'tanka, the Great Power, has meant it to be this way?"

Many talks followed, considering the real meaning of this happening. The head chief closed the council saying, "Surely Wakan'tanka must have arranged something for the Sioux Nation. It has taken one year before the horse was taken, and I say let us take one whole year to make plans against the Raven People. They are not many, but they are shrewd and tricky in battle. The time has come that we must destroy them. But first we must take time to make plans."

The graver crisis at hand for the Dakota bands, however, was the coming of the whites in such numbers. They were rapidly decimating the buffalo herds and desecrating their sacred mountains, the Black Hills, with diggings for the yellow metal. Their hunting grounds had been getting smaller and smaller, with fewer and fewer food animals. They had to find new grounds. To the west was a vast area still teeming with buffalo, deer, antelope, and other game, and it was still free from molestation by the whites. Only the Crows lived there, and they were not many.

Later that fall another council was called. It was here decided that all the bands of the great Dakota Nation and the

Cheyenne and Arapaho be invited to join Brave Wolf in a great undertaking. Teams of two men were selected as emissaries to all the other bands with instructions to stay with these people for the winter. They were to gradually influence the bands to participate in what they would describe as a grand venture to move into the good country of their traditional enemies, the Absarokee.

The emissaries did their work well during the winter. By the next May all the Dakota bands, the Cheyenne, and the Arapahos began coming to the designated place of gathering—the forks of Big Goose Creek and Little Goose Creek, where Sheridan, Wyoming, now stands. As the bands arrived and set up their tepees, the encampment grew larger and larger. It was said that camp criers had to change mounts several times before making a complete circle around the entire encampment. This was probably the largest gathering of Indians at any one time in North America. Sitting Bull's famously "large" camp on the Little Bighorn River some sixteen years later would be lost from sight in this gigantic camp at the forks of Goose Creek.

In the meantime, scouts came back and reported that the Crows were camped in Pass Creek, only a half-day's ride to the north. The war chiefs of the bands and the Cheyenne and Arapaho allies quickly gathered in council. Time was of prime importance as their common enemy was moving away quite rapidly; their scouts had probably seen the big camp at Goose Creek. One by one the band chiefs spoke about the impending battle.

The Arapaho chief was asked to speak. He was tall and impressive in appearance. He said, "The Dakota people and their Cheyenne friends know me as Night Horse, Arapaho chief. Other tribes also know me. I fear no man of any enemy tribe. I am an Absarokee by birth, and I will not fight my own relatives. This is not Indian war you are planning. To destroy another tribe is wrong. I don't want any part of it. However, I give permission to my warriors to stay and fight with you if they desire. You have heard me, Aho!"

That same day Night Horse broke camp and departed, heading for the Bighorn Mountains to the southwest. He quickly dispatched his two half-Crow sons to warn the Crow camp of the war expedition massed against them by thousands of Sioux, Cheyenne, and Arapahos bent on destroying the whole Absarokee people.

In the meantime, the Crows broke camp rapidly and headed west. By evening they were camping by Rotten Grass Creek, a day's travel from Pass Creek, when Night Horse's sons arrived. Immediately they were surrounded by alert Crow warriors, but when one spoke some Crow words and said they were the sons of Night Horse, they were escorted to the lodge of the head chief. A Crow who could speak in the Arapaho language explained to the Crow chief and his elders that a huge army of Dakotas and their Cheyenne allies were only a day's ride behind them. Night Horse's advice was that this small camp of Crows move away as fast as possible and join with other camps of Crow bands.

The chief listened, but others said, "We shouldn't listen to these sneaky Arapahos; they are up to some trick," or "We Crows are not all women, and we don't run away from the Dakotas," and such remarks. Finally the head chief told the half-Crow messengers they would think over the information they had brought. A wise elder interrupted: "These boys have ridden a long way; what they have told us must be true. Even our own scouts know about the big hostile camp. We must leave and travel fast."

Tepees were taken down hastily, horses packed, and soon the Absarokee were on their way. The evening camp was set up on the west side of the Bighorn River. Horses were tied, equipment unpacked, and everything readied for a quick departure the next morning at daybreak.

While the Crows were making the fast march toward the Bighorn River, there was great activity in the camp at Goose Creek: Warriors busily packed their horses, women prepared packs of extra moccasins and pemmican snacks for their men, and boys played at being warriors. As the great horde of warriors started out, there was much gaiety. Wives sang farewell songs and shrilled encouragement, warriors whooped war cries, and old men sang praise songs. At the head of the mighty procession was Brave Wolf himself, riding the prancing roan with his double-trailer war bonnet fluttering behind. He was indeed magnificent, the very image of a great Dakota warrior.

The Sioux storyteller recalled that many noncombatants joined the march, mainly wives and girlfriends of the warriors and many old and retired warriors who wanted to see the utter defeat of their traditional enemy. He said he decided to go, too. While he was taking the liberty of "borrowing" his brother's buffalo-hunting horse, his sister-in-law discovered him and scolded him harshly: "You leave that horse alone. With it your brother brings meat. You are not worthy of even touching that horse!" He said he slunk away to get his only horse, a slow and lazy one, and followed the already departed group. He went on to say that he was going mainly to look on and see the annihilation of the Absarokee. He added that he felt safe with so many good warriors along.

The advance scouts reported that the Crows were camped at the Bighorn River a short distance below the canyon. At once the head chiefs decided to attack the Crow camp, consisting of about four hundred lodges, at dawn the following morning, but at daybreak the Crows were gone, the camp-fires still smoldering. Here the chief in command motioned his men to stop. He wanted to estimate the size of the Crow fighting force. He would allocate ten Sioux warriors, each armed with guns, to every Crow tepee site. Even after all the lodge sites had been allocated in that way, the remaining warriors were a larger group, all bearing guns, bows and arrows, spears, and tomahawks. At this the chief smiled and shouted, "Wash-tay!" (good), and the warriors let out a thundering war whoop that shook the nearby Bighorn Mountains! The chief shrilled, "Today when the sun sets, there will be no more Absarokee left! We will kill all their warriors and even the old men; we will save their young boys and raise them to become Dakota warriors, and we shall marry their wives and daughters to raise more warriors to fight the whites when they follow us to our new land."

The commander quickly estimated, on the basis of three Crow warriors for each lodge, that the Absarokee were outnumbered at least twenty-five to one (twelve hundred Crows against eight to ten thousand Sioux and allied warriors). It has been said that this was the first time in Sioux history that all the bands came together to wage war against a common enemy. Moreover, it's never happened since. Not even Sitting Bull was able to muster so many warriors on the Little Bighorn sixteen years later.

When Joe Childs finished his smoke, he recalled that many times he and his father, Child in the Mouth, would sit at the same spot and relive that glorious day in the history of the Crow Indians.

Joe Childs explained that when Night Horse's sons came and warned the Crows, the decision was made to hasten far into the interior of the Crow country where the other Mountain Crow camp was. At that time of early morning when "one can begin to see the lines in his palm," the four hundred lodges on the Bighorn were taken down and packed on horses. Soon the horses were in a fast trot. That evening the travelers reached Pryor Creek, about fifty miles to the west. At sunset the Crows were still very much alive. Their hostile pursuers couldn't catch up and had to wait another day to do what they had come out to do.

The events of the fateful following day began quickly and dramatically. At early dawn a Crow man named Hits Himself Over the Head was searching for his horses when he suddenly came up a hill to look over upon a seething mass of men and horses. The scene was one of bustling activity, as warriors got their war horses ready, put on their battle regalia, and were about to mount and charge down the hill toward the Crows. Hits Himself ducked out of sight and raced for the Crow camp. As he approached he hollered the warning call, and the head chiefs were already gathered to hear his report. Immediately they dispatched ten gallant warriors toward the enemy to hold off the initial charge just long enough to set up battle lines and to put up a fortress of tepee poles and covers, which the women were busy doing.

The ten men charged right into the enemy and fired into the ranks, killing a number of Sioux. As they swerved to return, thousands of warriors roared down the hills in hot pursuit, truly a thundering charge. And seen at its head was a warrior on a dark roan horse wearing a war bonnet with two streamers flying behind. As they approached the creek, the pursuers halted. Brave Wolf crossed the creek and headed directly to the first line of defense already set by the Crow war chiefs. But about halfway there Brave Wolf suddenly changed his mind and turned to flee. At this moment two Crows took pursuit. One noted for his accuracy with the bow caught up with the Dakota warrior and sent an arrow into him. As he tumbled to the ground, the other Crow pursuer jumped off his horse, quickly scalped the fallen Brave Wolf, waved the trophy at the Sioux, and gestured that he would do the same to many of them that day.

Thus the long-awaited day for exterminating the Absarokee began. Suddenly the small valley exploded with war whoops, gunfire, and the thunder of thousands of horses' hooves beating the ground. The followers of the war party now sat in clusters here and there on a high escarpment near the battle scene. While some men smoked the pipe, the women sang victory songs and emitted shrills of encouragement to their fighting men below.

My storyteller, Joe Childs, now on his feet, launched into a lively and excited description of the fight as if he were right there at the real battle! He pointed to an open flat area and said that was where the Crows had set up their first line of defense. Crow warriors noted for their fine marksmanship with guns and bows took a similar position nearby. As the enemy crossed the creek and charged, one of the veteran Crow chiefs gave a loud command, and the Crows opened a concerted fire with deadly results. Quickly the Dakotas regrouped and made another charge, again suffering heavy casualties. When this happened several times, the ferocity of the Sioux attackers dwindled, and the Crows commenced launching their own offensive charges.

It may be explained at this point that for this particular encounter—a clear life-or-death situation—the Crow war chiefs adopted the strategy of warriors working together as a team under the direction of a war chief; the traditional display of bravery, where individuals would charge into the enemy ranks trying to count coups by striking an enemy with a stick, was put aside.

The repeated charges by the Dakotas suddenly stopped. The Crows waited and wondered. Then a wise Crow Indian decided to take advantage of the lull to try a bluff, hoping to instill fear into the hearts of the attackers. He rode toward the enemy making the sign that he had something to say. This often happened in Plains Indian warfare. Through the intertribal sign language, he said: "You have come a long way. By the size of your party, you have come prepared to wage serious battle against the Absarokee this day. You are not an ordinary war party this time. Yes, the Raven People will fight you in a great way. Right now our two other bands are on their way to help us. They will arrive soon, and then you will have a real fight on your hands. I have spoken, Aho, Aho!"

The truth was, no help was coming at all. But the bluff was quickly followed by strange happenings. As the Crow was returning to his ranks, the Sioux onlookers on the hill were on their feet pointing excitedly toward the north; then they waved frantically and shouted to their warriors below that a large war party was coming up the creek. At this moment it so happened that a large herd of elk had become excited by the noises of battle and had started milling around. Their sharp hooves stirred a swirling cloud of dust. Their white rumps looked like war bonnets!

Again the ones on the hill hollered—another war party was fast approaching from the west. This time the warriors could plainly see a huge cloud of dust moving rapidly toward the battleground. This phenomenon was caused by a large herd of stampeding buffalo frightened by the noise of battle in the valley.

And now there was feverish excitement as groups of Dakota warriors milled around. The Sioux war chiefs quickly ordered a determined charge, hoping to dislodge the Crow defense lines before help arrived. Once again the lines held and inflicted heavy casualties.

At this time, a third strange thing took place. Now the Sioux saw a lone warrior riding hard from the hills to join the Crow defenders. He was mounted on a dark horse with white markings on its flanks. His weapon was a two-pronged spear made of elk antler. Suddenly this mystic warrior hollered, "Kokohay! Kokohay!" and charged. He was followed by several Crow warriors. The man charged right into a group and began spearing Sioux warriors right and left. Other groups stood their ground and opened fire with many guns. Their shots were harmless; the man was invulnerable to bullets and arrows. He would circle and return, repeating the one-man onslaught. At this time the Crow ranks holding the defense lines broke loose into a full charge. The Sioux and their Cheyenne and Arapaho allies gave ground, before long breaking into a full retreat, with every man for himself. The strange Crow warrior was right behind them, shouting, "Kokohay! Kokohay!" and continuing to wield his deadly spear.

Here I will digress and take up Charles Ten Bear's Sioux version, as told by the one who tagged along on the slow horse just to watch the battle. This man explained to Ten Bear that just before the charge into Pryor Creek Valley, his brother handed him one of the two extra horses he had brought along. This horse was fast and long-winded. So he decided to get into the battle about the time the Crows started to counterattack. He recalled that he decided to retreat as fast as his horse could run. Then the horse started to weave and to lose speed; soon he could see blood spattering from the horse's mouth; then it rolled over, dead.

Now he was afoot and could hear, "Kokohay! Kokohay!" not far behind him. He thought he would surely die. But very fortunately he saw a Sioux horse trotting by, dragging the reins. He succeeded in catching the horse, which he recognized as the fastest and most durable horse of the Sioux, and escaped. He joined a group and hastened back toward the big camp at the forks of Goose Creek. Whenever they stopped for a short rest in the dark, suddenly they would hear, "Kokohay! Kokohay!" above them in the sky. On they would go.

The Sioux storyteller related to Charles Ten Bear that when his group reached the base camp on Goose Creek, already there was wailing throughout the camp. After two days of waiting, when no more warriors returned, the various bands dispersed. He said his own band moved southward to Big Piney Creek, about a half-day's travel, and camped for the night. Camp criers cautioned the people to be alert. Not long after the campfires were put out, the silence was suddenly broken with Crow war whoops and gunfire. A rider (the Crow war chief Hillside) ran his horse through a Sioux lodge where a woman was in labor. The horse stepped on the woman and child, killing them instantly. No one slept that night. Early the following day the band fled toward the Black Hills and camped at Crazy Woman Creek, not far from the Powder River. Here again the camp criers warned everyone to stay inside the tepees after dark. But one old man had to go outside to relieve himself. While he was crouched, a colt looking for its mother came behind him quietly and nudged him with a wet nose. The poor old man screamed, collapsed, and died. He was the one hundredth casualty.

Charles Ten Bear's Sioux informant estimated that about one hundred Sioux and Cheyenne warriors failed to return from the land of the Absarokee. Many were killed in action on Pryor Creek, while others may have been killed by grizzly bears or drowned in the wide and swift Bighorn River.

After the era of intertribal warfare on the Plains—which ended with the battle of the Little Bighorn of June 1876 and with Chief Joseph's surrender at the Bears Paw Mountains in 1877—the Plains tribes would visit back and forth among the various Indian reservations. Indian agents would issue visitation passes. Here the tribal historians of the different tribes would exchange information and verify in detail all the facts pertaining to a particular battle. In this way many great Indian-to-Indian battles were recorded in the memories of tribal historians and storytellers.

On one occasion, some Sioux came to visit the Crows. Among other inquiries, the visitors wanted to know the name of the ferocious warrior who almost single-handedly stampeded the Sioux and Cheyenne that day at Pryor Creek. The Crow historians, some of them veterans of the Pryor Creek battle themselves, could not recall such a warrior among the Crows that day. There was absolutely no recollection of such a person as described by the Sioux, even though the Sioux insisted that he had been there that day.

After hearing about the mystery warrior from the Sioux, Crow historians finally came up with an explanation. It was recalled that during the height of the Sioux attack, an old Crow woman came out of the fortification, walked to a point where she could see the enemy, stood, and prayed: "Old Man Coyote, teacher and benefactor of the Absarokee people, one day you made a promise. You said that after you had been gone from us for some time, if one day the people should be in great danger, that you would come back to help us. You said that we should pray for your quick return. I now pray for you to come and help us survive this very day. Come, come!"

It was believed that the woman's prayer was answered when Old Man Coyote, the Great Spirit's helper to the Absarokee, suddenly appeared in the form of a special warrior and stampeded the enemy. It was also believed that it was Old Man Coyote's help that caused the elk and buffalo herds to mill around, raising clouds of dust that looked like fast-approaching relief. Perhaps Night Horse was right when he said to the war chiefs at Goose Creek that the plan to exterminate another tribe, the Absarokee, was wrong and a bad thing.

Today this story is known by a few Crows. At one time, traditional storytellers kept the story alive. The Sioux and Cheyenne seldom, if ever, talked about the humiliating defeat at Pryor Creek. Their story has been almost completely lost in secrecy since that day in the 1860s.

A CROW AND GROS VENTRE BATTLE

In the mid-1860s, some Crows and Gros Ventres (Atsina) met in battle at the confluence of the Little Bighorn River and Lodge Grass Creek (Greasy Grass), where the community of Lodge Grass, Montana, now stands. The Crows refer to this event as "When the Enemy Was Counter-Attacked."

One evening, it was reported that a large war party was coming up the Little Bighorn Valley and setting up a bivouac camp at the "Bend of the Cliffs" (where George Hogan now lives, about eight miles north of Lodge Grass). A war council was immediately called to hear the report. The hunters who saw the enemy insisted that it was a large party, sufficient in size to endanger the Crow camp. The question was whether to move camp or to stay and fight. One chief suggested that the renowned scout His Medicine Is the Wolf personally go and ascertain the enemy's strength. The scout left at once.

The council was still in session when the scout returned and reported that the enemy was none other than the foolhardy Hairy Nostrils. They were indeed in sufficient force to overrun the Crow camp. It was decided quickly that the best strategy would be to take the offensive and strike first!

Well before daybreak, the Crow warriors were on their way. Apparently, the enemy was likewise on the move and about halfway the two parties unexpectedly ran into each other. The battle was on. After the first flurry of disorganized, man-to-man, pitched fighting, the parties withdrew and reorganized. As one side charged, the other side retreated, and vice versa; the skirmish line moved back and forth. That day, the Hairy Nostrils were the aggressors and by late afternoon the Crows found themselves at the edge of their camp. In a desperation charge, they broke the enemy line and chased the invaders up the nearby hills overlooking the valley. Here the Hairy Nostrils reassembled, held an impromptu scalp or victory dance, and disappeared.

After the era of intertribal warfare, when historians of both tribes met to review and corroborate the true account of this battle, the Crows asked why the Hairy Nostrils held a victory dance on the hill when so many of their warriors had been killed. They replied that "it was because we pushed you back into your camp." The Crow considered this reply typical of the Hairy Nostrils, who often displayed unusual and unexpected acts, even on the battlefield.

THE CROW CONCEPT OF VISION QUEST

The quiet and mystic serenity of the Wolf Teeth Mountains has always provided the good and right setting for vision seeking. Some of the prominences in the mountains display physical evidence where clandestine and lonely worship took place, where man sought communion with his Maker and wished to receive the *Baxbe*, or Power.

The Absarokee, surrounded and besieged on all sides by hostile tribes, was by necessity a tribe of superb warriors physically, mentally, and spiritually. The Crow believed that by fasting he could obtain supernatural power through animal emissaries of the First Maker (or Great Spirit). He believed that this power would make him a better warrior, more successful in performing war deeds, helping him to eventually become a chief with great wealth, high prestige, and a large following.

The Crow called this spiritual experience "Going Without Water." It was basically a fasting supplication. Through suffering from exposure to the elements, from the pangs of thirst and hunger, and from the pain of blood sacrifice (cutting off a finger and bleeding into unconsciousness), the faster hoped to gain the pity of the animal spirits (the Ones Without Fires). Thus to receive an early "visit" by them and to be given instructional dreams and visions were the sure signs of "receiving the Baxbe, the Sacred Power."

The ordeal was not mandatory; it was voluntary. While nearly all young men, but particularly the aspiring warriors, believed that they needed to have a personal vision experience, some preferred to go directly to a veteran warrior or chief with a proven and recognized Baxbe ("medicine," as the white man called it) and to obtain his "blessings" by paying a certain fee.

The rows of stones or slabs of rocks, usually oblong-shaped, used by those "Going Without Water" were made not for comfort but as symbolic beds. The names for these structures, therefore, suggest this concept: "fasting bed," "where someone had lain," "where to dream," and "where to have visions" are examples.

The two most common types of fasting bed are the open oblong and the closed oblong. With the former, the open end faces the east so that "the blessings of the morning sun may enter directly" upon the seeker. The closed bed may be oriented in any direction, and presumably the faster would be up before sunrise. In both types, the height of the walls varies from only a few inches to more than a foot.

Two Leggings, one of the last Crow chiefs, explained that a faster would build the walls high enough so that by placing strong limbs or small poles across them, a platform could be made. On this platform, pine boughs were placed, to be used as a bed during the day and to crawl under at night or in bad weather. This arrangement was no doubt the exception, because the Crow faster deliberately set out to endure discomfort and to suffer actual physical pain by cutting off a finger at the first joint and offering a blood sacrifice to the First Maker, with the Grandfather (the sun) as witness. It was hoped that such suffering would move the animal spirits and emissaries to pity and to visit the supplicant.

Some vision seekers did not bother to build beds but moved from place to place. Women mourners doing penance and staying outside the camp for a period of time also did not use beds, even though there was a distinct element of fasting in their ordeal.

The selection of sites for fasting was an individual matter. A faster might set his bed on a bare open hilltop, under a tree, in among trees, on a precarious ledge of a high cliff, on an island in a lake or river, or at a place he believed likely to attract the spirits, the dispensers of the Baxbe. And upon the advice of a clan uncle or a medicine man, he might even use the same bed once used by a person who had had a good vision there.

Most vision quest sites are singles, but occasionally two are placed together a short distance apart. A vision quest site located at the headwaters of Grey Blanket Creek originally consisted of two beds spaced a few feet apart. During World War II, two men from Lodge Grass rearranged the stones and fasted there. On Dryhead Overlook in the Pryor Mountains, a sacred fasting grounds for the Absarokee, many fasting beds can be seen even today. A row of seven, a few rods apart, are acknowledged to be the ones used by Plenty Coups, Medicine Crow, Two Leggings, and four other young men in the 1860s. In 1973, four new ones were made and used there by young Crows preparing for an upcoming tribal Sun Dance ceremony.

On the Northern Cheyenne Reservation, adjoining the Crow Reservation on the east side, there is a large site about ten feet in diameter and about three feet high where, it has been related, seven Cheyenne men fasted simultaneously. This multiple fasting practice seems to suggest that the famed Medicine Wheel in the Bighorn Mountains in northern Wyoming was perhaps originally structured as a mass fasting place. The six, possibly seven, cairns placed along the rim of the circle may be fasting beds.

It can be stated, therefore, that in the classical Crow Indian vision-seeking fast there were no rules or customs forbidding plural or group fasting in close proximity.

In conclusion, the Crow Indians have been depending upon and using the Wolf Mountains as a place where good and true dreams and visions can be obtained. Truly, these hills have been sacred to the Crows. It is said that Red Woman of Crow mythology once lived here and may still be here in spirit. As a young man, Twines His [horse's] Tail, the great River Crow chief, fasted one whole summer along the Wolf Teeth without success. On his last bed atop the highest and southernmost tip of the mountain overlooking the Tongue River, though, Twines His Tail experienced an overwhelming visitation and was "adopted" by none other than the Grandfather, the sun. He became a great medicine man and head chief of the entire Crow tribe for many years. Another famed Crow, Red Plume at Forehead (also known as Long Hair, the chief written about and ex-tolled by early white traders and explorers), fasted on a high point at the headwaters of Owl Creek in the Wolf Teeth. He was "adopted" by the Morning Star and received a power-ful vision. He also became a great head chief and medicine man.

PILES OF STONE

Rock piles or mounds of intentionally placed stones appear to have been associated mainly with intertribal warfare. The rather small rock piles located at seemingly random places were markers for Crow warriors killed or for enemies killed in warring incidents. When a noted Crow warrior or chief was killed, the marker would in time become a shrine; peo-ple would visit the site and add rocks as a sign of respect. Alternatively, such a site might be considered "haunted" and avoided. The pile of rocks indicating the exact spot where Yellow Leggings was killed at the north end of the Wolf Mountains is a case in point.

At important battlefields, there would be erected any

number of markers, either for killed Crow warriors or for indicating the place where a noteworthy feat was performed by a Crow combatant. In the 1850s and mid-1860s, large-scale battles with invading Sioux took place where the present community of Wyola, Montana, now stands. It is recalled that before farming began, quite a number of rock mounds were seen there; many may have been removed or destroyed long ago.

At Pryor Gap, there is still clearly visible a neat row of stone piles that commemorates the place where a big battle took place a "very long time ago," according to Crow tribal history. This row of stone piles has become a tribal shrine. For many years, the Crow people passing that way have added rocks and offered prayers for their safe passage and return. Such "wishing well" cairns are generally found at favorite mountain passes. No example of this type is known in the Wolf Mountains.

Until a farmer broke the sod there and the landmark was destroyed, a marker could be found a short distance from the last mound on the north end of the Pryor Gap row indicating where Medicine Crow rode in between two fleeing Arapaho horsemen and brought them down just as his horse was shot. In this instance, the marker was a hero's monument rather than a headstone.

About one-quarter mile southwest and across the creek from the southernmost pile are two or three larger rock piles at the foot of Arrow Rock. Here the Crows would offer rocks and beads to the mythological Little People, who had once occupied the caves here. Men would often offer arrows by shooting them high into the crevasses in the cliffs. These mounds are not related to the nearby row of rock piles.

Rock piles, mounds, and cairns are not only intriguing in themselves, but they are easily subject to modification and to the creation of new variations as modern people get into the act. Ego monuments constructed by sheepherders and cowboys, surveyors' cornerstones, and miners' claims are some of their contributions to the profusion of above-ground stone structures. Mounded stones associated with buffalo surround and drive sites are rather easily distinguished from the kinds of piled stone discussed above. The widely dispersed, small, individual piles of stone found in the Wolf Mountains area are not readily explained by the kinds of experiences known to the living Crows.

Crow Indian Buffalo Jumps

~~~~~~~~~~~~~~~~~~~~

A Study and Analysis of Techniques Used in Luring, Driving, and Stampeding Buffalo Over Cliffs

HISTORICAL REFERENCES

The Crow Indian name or term for the so-called bison jump is "Driving Buffalo Over Embankments." With the exception of one legendary account, all presently known references to this particular method of meat procurement are historical, with actual names given to the sites and to the individuals involved. The Cheyenne and Shoshoni Indians, who apparently had no traditions of bison jumping, secretly observed the Crows conducting jumps and subsequently adopted the technique and used the same cliffs favored by the Crows.

1. According to legend, Old Man Coyote, the culture teacher of the Crows and Hidatsa, first taught the people how to kill many buffalo by tricking a herd over a hidden cliff. Presumably from that time until the early 1870s, the

Crow Indians practiced this method of mass slaughter of bison.

2. Running Coyote, a contemporary of Chief No Vitals who led a seceding faction of the ancestral tribe out west about 1600–25, was credited as the first Crow to have originated the technique of stampeding buffalo over embankments. This was probably in the mid-1600s, while the seceding band was migrating westward.

3. Chief One Heart, who lived in the "stone and bone tool days," often used the mass-slaughter technique of chasing buffalo onto ice-slicks at drinking places. His favorite places were along the lower Yellowstone River. It is said that he would employ a number of good runners to chase and stampede a herd toward the slaughter site. This chief probably lived and ruled around the turn of the eighteenth century, before the acquisition of firearms and horses.

4. Chief Tip of Fur engineered a spontaneous stampede of buffalo over a cliff at the confluence of Hoodoo Creek and Dryhead Creek about 1865. After the butchering the chief ordered that all the severed heads be piled at the foot of the cliff. This site was used on several occasions afterward, and in time there was a vast accumulation of skulls or dried heads at this place. The Crows called this site "Place of Many Dry Heads" and for this reason the creek was eventually called Dryhead Creek. A woman by the name of Big Medicine Rock witnessed Tip of Fur's buffalo kill and would often tell the story to her grandson Martin He Does It. This woman died in 1924.

5. Plain Feather, who died in 1970 at the age of one hundred, also told of a spontaneous jump that his mother witnessed in the late 1860s. This happened at Pryor Creek where Highway 87, locally known as the Old Hardin Road, crosses the creek. Plain Feather recalled that when he was

a young man his mother pointed out the rimrocks where Crow hunters once chased and crowded a small herd of buffalo over sandstone cliffs. A cow was wedged in a crevasse, and the bones remained there for a long time.

6. "Where Buffaloes Are Driven Over Cliffs at Long Ridge" was a favorite meat-procurement place for Crow Indians for well more than a century (say early 1700s to 1870). This site was located on a tributary creek of the Yellowstone south of what is now Livingston, Montana. There is no doubt that this is the Emigrant Jump Site on Findley Creek.

According to Charles Ten Bear, a Crow historian who died in the mid-1960s, the Crows used this place every fall. He explained that there were two places or cliffs at the point of a long ridge sloping to the creek, and these would be used simultaneously. What animals escaped the upper cliff were generally caught on the second or lower one.

Ten Bear went on to relate that the tribe would come and camp near the Long Ridge in the fall. The night before the drive and jump, a council would be held and the participants were selected, some to drive the herd from the rear and a few to haze near the jump-off point. Sometimes dogs were used on the drive. A medicine man was also asked to officiate. Early in the morning this medicine man would stand on the edge of the upper cliff, facing up the ridge. He would take a pair of hindquarters, point the feet along the line of stones, and sing his sacred songs calling upon the Great Spirit to make the operation a success. After this invocation the medicine man would give the two head drivers a pouch of incense. As the two head drivers and their helpers headed up the ridge along the line of stones, they would stop and burn incense on the ground, repeating the process four times. As the two groups reached the top, they would form a line and start down the ridge. All the animals along the ridge would be chased down the hill, including buffalo, deer, elk, bighorn sheep, and even small animals. The mysterious thing about this is that the animals would come to the line where incense was burned and bolt back into the ridge area. Apparently there was little or no deployment of hazers along the incense line except near the cliff. Here the rock piles are higher, larger, and closer together for hazers to take some protection.

7. What the Crow Indians regarded as their very own "butcher shop" was located in the Grapevine Creek drainage basin, which empties into the Bighorn River about one and one-half miles below Yellowtail Dam. This area is still called by the Crows "Where Men Pack [get] Meat" or "Where Men Always Find Game." This large basin is enclosed by a high escarpment on the north, the high walls of Bighorn River Canyon on the south, and rimrocks with a narrow gap on the east, and has all the ingredients for great buffalo jumping. With good grass, ample water, and an elevation ideally suited for all-summer grazing, buffalo, as well as deer and elk, were always here for the taking.

With little effort a small group of Crow hunters could always and easily execute a jump and procure whatever amount of meat and hides was needed at the time. The jumps and guideline rocks or lanes were so arranged that two or three sites could be used simultaneously. In addition to the regular drive lanes, there are many rock lines that simply have no apparent connection with the established jump sites. Presumably these were used for winter driving and foundering of bison into deep and narrow gullies, which are numerous here.

In all probability the Crows constructed many of these jump sites soon after their arrival here in the early eighteenth century and continued to add to and improve the system until the end of buffalo-hunting days about 1880. Even in the early 1900s Crow youths enjoyed using a particularly deceptive jump site to kill elk and deer. It is also possible that the Shoshoni and Flatheads may have made some of the jumps before the arrival of the Crows.

I was shown three sites in the early 1960s and shortly thereafter two or three more were found. At present there are close to twenty jump sites here within a radius of two to three miles. Several types of jumps and drive lines are found here. Some are the classical V-shaped lines leading to a cliff; others have just one line but utilize a natural barrier for the other side. Some lines are short and some are nearly two miles long. There are other features that are difficult to explain, such as little or no bone deposits at the bottom of the jump cliffs and the presence of very few tepee rings.

8. John Stands in Timber, the late Northern Cheyenne historian, related to me that when the Cheyenne first came into this area (about the turn of the nineteenth century), they would secretly watch the Crows running a jump on one of the western tributaries of the Tongue River (St. John's Creek). Later they tried their own operation at the same site with good success and often used the site thereafter. Stands in Timber explained that when the tribe lived in the Black Hills area they had a system of herding antelope into pits, but they did not use it with buffalo.

9. Herman St. Clair, a Shoshoni of Ft. Washakie, Wyoming, also related a similar account. He told me that in the 1860s the Shoshoni witnessed the Crows doing a jump at Heart Mountain west of what is now Cody, Wyoming. The Shoshoni called this place "Painted Cliff." They also experimented and succeeded in stampeding a good herd over the cliff and thereafter used the site several times. This

informant stated that the Shoshoni had a system of driving bighorn sheep and goats into compounds but never buffalo until they learned the jump from the Crows.

CONCLUSIONS

The accounts given above together with available ethno-historical data on buffalo jumping lead me to make the following concluding remarks:

1. It was during No Vitals's westward migration that the stampeding of bison over cliffs was invented. A man named Running Coyote was credited as the originator of the technique. Legends indicate that prior to the division and separation of the ancestral tribe about 1600–25, hunters were familiar with animal surrounds.

2. As the first of the migrating tribes from the eastern woodlands to enter this area (southern Montana and northern Wyoming), it may be presumed that the Crows or Absarokee must have built or rebuilt and used the majority of the jump sites in this area. Certainly Crows have oral traditions concerning the Emigrant, Grapevine, Keogh, and other sites. The fact that Cheyenne and Shoshoni witnessed and adopted Crow jumping operations supports this conclusion.

3. Several types of jump sites are discernible, and the manner or method of their use varied according to accounts of eyewitnesses as well as deductions derived after careful study of the location of the jump cliff, the surrounding terrain, the arrangement of the line of stones, and other relevant features. The types are as follows:

A. The distinctive feature of the Classical type of jump is the V-shaped line of stones emanating from the edge of the cliff for a distance of a few yards to more than two miles. The point of the V at the rim of the cliff may be as narrow as a few feet or as wide as six, seven, or eight yards. The Madison or Logan, Emigrant, and Dryhead Ranch jump sites and several in the Grapevine area are good examples of this type. (See Figure 1.) The operation of this type of jump featured the special role of a medicine man as described in Charles Ten Bear's account of Crow Indians' us-

FIGURE 1

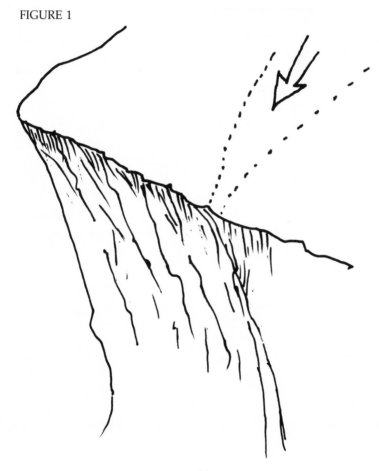

ing the Emigrant site. Let us consider two points that are difficult to understand. First, only a few men, perhaps less than a dozen, were used, mainly as drivers at the rear of the downhill movement of the animals rather than as hazers on the sides along the so-called drive lines; and second, the animals, including elk, deer, and bighorn sheep, when trying to escape to the right or left, would abruptly halt and bolt back upon approaching the "incense line." To explain these points is not easy. Other than concluding that the smell of the incense itself repelled the animals back into the onrushing herd, one may simplistically dismiss the matter by saying that the medicine man's power was indeed good and strong! The Cheyenne, when living in the Black Hills area in the early 1800s, often conducted antelope drives into pit compounds. It is said that after the medicine man blessed the operation, no animals could escape and even birds within the drive area would not be able to fly out. This, of course, is not a scientific explanation, and it is not acceptable to anthropologists. But the Indians themselves pragmatically accepted the phenomenon because it worked, and therefore they believed it must be true. Surely the medicine man did his work well!

I may further conjecture here that at the Classical sites the V line of cantaloupe-size stones were mainly markers where the medicine man's incense was burned and not "drive lines" where it is generally presumed that people would hide and haze the herd on toward the jump cliff. This is not saying that hazers were not used at all.

B. What may be regarded as an Intermediate type of jump site is one that combines one man-made line of stones with another side utilizing a natural barrier like an escarpment. (See Figure 2, page 94.) The use of this type of site would be somewhat opposite to the operation at a Classical site;

here there would be the deployment of many individuals and a minimum of the medicine man's doings. Some verbal accounts indicate that the entire camp population participated, while a few fast runners worked as rear drivers and as side hazers. The hazers taking positions along the stone markers would hold up robes between individuals, thus forming a "human fence," waving and shouting as the drive accelerated. Yelping dogs would also add to the effective-

FIGURE 2

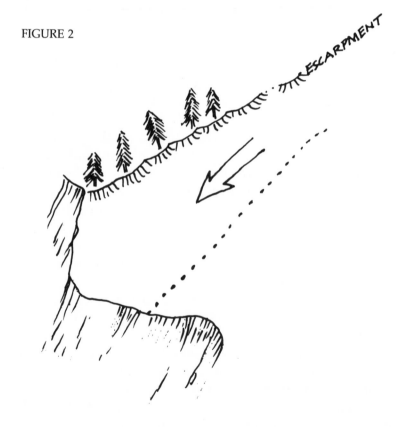

ness of the human line. These Intermediate sites in the Grapevine Complex generally have rather formidable piles of stones near the edge of the jump cliff, so the intrepid hazers stationed here would have protection.

C. A third type of site is the Natural, where no man-made structures were used. Generally these are either deceptive trails leading to hidden cliffs or a high-walled, peninsula-like bench (see Figure 3) or point onto which a herd of grazing bison could be quickly trapped. These jump sites, camouflaged by nature, were used spontaneously when hunters found a herd near such places and could easily spook, trap, and stampede the herd over the embankment. Such operations were never planned; hunters on hand at the right moment would execute the jump whether afoot or on horseback. Some of the Grapevine sites and the Hoodoo-

FIGURE 3

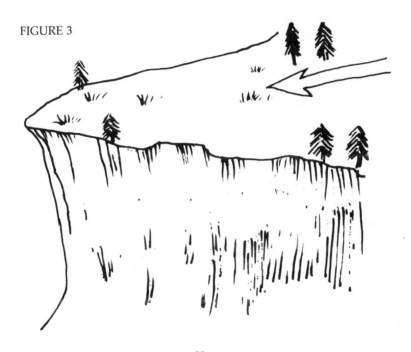

Dryhead site were of this type and were often used when conditions were right.

D. A Combination type consists of two or three adjoining and interrelated sites. These are arranged in such a layout that one, two, or all three could be simultaneously put into operation, much like an automatic shotgun where the trigger could be pulled as many times as needed. The Emigrant site and at least two in Grapevine are two-jump combinations, and another one in Grapevine is a three-jump variety. The multijump sites could be any combination of the above-mentioned types. The three-jumper in Grapevine is a Classical, Intermediate, and Natural combination! (See Figure 4.) This is probably the most sophisticated bison jump anywhere.

E. And there are places where piles of "old" buffalo bones are found that have no association whatsoever with any known man-made device of entrapment. These are mainly natural hazards along watering trails into which buffaloes fell from crowding and eventually died.

4. At Emigrant and at other sites, the presence and recovery of many so-called bird points is often confusing and a mystery to archaeologists. The bird point concept has been on the books too long. It is based on the analogy that in modern firearms small-caliber ammunition is used for small animals and birds and large-caliber for large animals.

A true "bird" arrow is not one with a small arrowhead attached to a shaft; it is one with a blunted or rounded tip, about the size of a medium walnut, of the arrow shaft itself. Such an arrow either stunned or killed the bird without tearing the meat. Such blunt-tipped arrows were also used to knock off arrows stuck high up in trees.

But back to the mystery of the recovery of many "bird

FIGURE 4

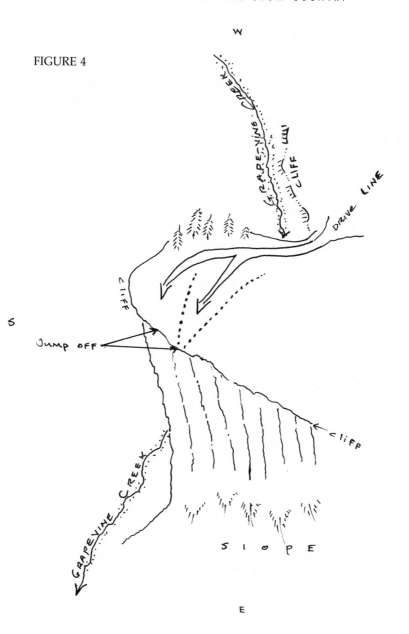

points" at some bison jump excavations. Besides the blunt points, the Crow Indians used two other types of arrows for hunting and warfare. Arrows with small points (so-called bird points), or with no points at all such as greasewood shafts with heat-hardened tips, were used mainly for quick and deep penetration of standing or motionless animals. Some bowmen were reputed to be able to send such arrows clear through animals, including the big buffalo, like steel-jacket bullets, with the same effects. For moving animals, especially buffalo chased on horseback, arrows with standard-size barbed heads were used. A hunter would send an arrow about six to eight inches into the soft flank just behind the ribs, and as the buffalo continued running, the arrow started cutting deeper and deeper into the vital organs; before long the animal stopped and soon died from internal hemorrhaging.

It may be surmised, therefore, that after a jump hunters finished off the wounded animals with the small-headed or plain greasewood arrows. Also it may be assumed that the larger heads or points became more useful and in demand after the acquisition of the horse and its subsequent use for buffalo hunting.

In warfare the larger barbed points were preferred because of their incapacitating effects. When a warrior was hit with such an arrow, it was less painful to extricate the arrow by pushing it through than by trying to pull it back out. A small-pointed arrow might go clear through a man and not mortally wound him if no vital organs or bones were hit.

5. Another mystery regarding the Grapevine Complex sites is the scarcity of bone deposits at some of the main jumps. A possible explanation for this is that many of the sites here were used mainly after the acquisition of the horse, and the hunters were therefore able to quarter the car-

casses and pack them off with horses to camps along the Bighorn River about two miles away. Also, those bones that were exposed were probably collected by bone hunters in the late 1920s, following the big horse-kill on the reservation earlier in the decade.

May I close with this statement: It is my belief that the Crow Indians used the cliff-jumping of bison more extensively and longer than any other tribe and that the greatest concentration of sites anywhere in North America is located in Grapevine Creek in the heart of the Crow country. The Grapevine Bison Jump Complex should be preserved, protected, and someday opened for interpretive display in its natural setting.

About Crow
Indian Horses

~~~~~~~~~~~~~~~~~~

A round 1725 or 1730 a Crow Indian war party journey-ed to the Fat River (Green River in Wyoming) and either purchased or stole a stallion horse from some other tribe and brought the animal back to the Crow camp in the Upper Wind River of what is now Wyoming.

This was quite an event because the Crows had never seen a horse before. It stood as high as an elk but looked very different, with round hooves, a long shaggy mane and tail, and no horns or antlers. As the people were looking it over, one man got too close to the hind legs of the animal. It quickly kicked him, and the man rolled over into the dirt. After this incident the pals of the man nicknamed him

Kicked in the Belly. In time this band of the Crow tribe came to be called Kicked in the Bellies. Today the descendants of these people live near Lodge Grass, Montana, and are still called by that name.

The same people, who live near Lodge Grass, have also been called "People of the Valley of Chieftains" because many great chiefs—such as Spotted Horse, Old Dog, Wolf Lays Down, and Medicine Crow—settled here when the Crow tribe ceded the western part of the reservation and moved to the eastern part in 1884.

About the same time as the Wind River horse incident, another story relates, a war party of the Mountain Crow band traveled south and brought back several of the new animals. This party apparently reached the Great Salt Lake.

Yet a third—and a highly mythical—version exists. In this story a Crow man saw strange animals in a dream. He set out looking for them and finally saw several emerging from a lake. He captured a few and brought them back to the Crow camp.

The usefulness of the new animal was quickly realized, and soon Crow war parties were heading south to bring back more horses. The Crows named this animal *Ichilay*, which means "to search with," perhaps referring to the search for enemies and game.

By 1743 when the La Vérendryes of the Hudson Bay Company met a small camp of Crow Indians east of the present town of Hardin, Montana, the Crows already owned many horses and were able to provide the traders with fresh mounts for their return.

Within a short time the Crows acquired large herds of horses by trading with other tribes, by stealing or capturing them from enemies, and by raising their own. Other tribes regarded the Absarokee as rich because they owned so many good horses. While other tribes used the travois to transport their equipment and people, the Crows all rode, from tiny tots to old people, and used packhorses. In this way they could travel fast over any kind of terrain.

The acquisition of the white-man's horse and firearms soon brought the formerly pedestrian nomads of the Plains into frequent contact and subsequent conflict as they invaded one another's territory and captured horses. Soon the tribes became more militaristic, and intertribal warfare became a way of life. These tribes developed similar military systems through which boys trained to become warriors and, by fulfilling military requirements, eventually attained the rank of chief. For the Crows, one of the four essential military tests was for a warrior to sneak into an enemy camp in darkness, capture a well-guarded, prized horse, and bring it home.

By the early 1800s the so-called Plains Indian Culture Area had come into existence, probably one of the last to develop in North America. A culture area is a geographic region inhabited by a number of tribes speaking different languages but sharing enough cultural traits to be classified as representing a distinct style of living.

With the Crow Indians, as with other Plains tribes, the horse quickly became an integral part of tribal culture. The horse has played an especially important role in Crow religion and social and economic life.

Religion. The Crows attributed to the horse, as to other animals, supernatural powers and regarded it as an emissary and agent of the Great Power. The Crow philosophy held that the Supreme Power had given all animals, the "Ones Without Fires," inherent supernatural powers that had not been given to human beings. Therefore man must obtain spiritual power through animal emissaries and revealers. Through a special dream or a vision or a fasting experience, an animal would come and prescribe to the supplicant the secret and sacred ways of using a particular gift—the power to heal certain sicknesses, to cure the wounded, to be invulnerable in battle, to prophesy, or to perform other mystical feats. Many Crow medicine men attributed their gift powers to the horse. These people were regarded as possessing "horse medicine." They were blessed with the strength, stamina, speed, and agility of the horse. Generally these individuals had an unusual propensity for finding and owning good horses, such as good warhorses, good buffalo-hunting horses, and fast racing horses; they could also cure sick horses, find horses when lost, and easily capture enemy horses.

A man with horse medicine had special songs about horses that he would sing in certain ceremonies and dances. Whenever he was asked to name a child, he would invariably use the word *horse* in the name. By so doing, he expressed a wish and prayer that the child would grow to live up to the meaning of the name. Among the Crows today there are many family names such as Takes a Horse, Rides a Horse, Good Horse, and so on.

Social Life. In many of the social customs and traditions of the Crow Indians, the horse played important roles.

• In the days of intertribal warfare, if a Crow warrior brought back horses, he would distribute them to his sisters and female cousins.

• After the days of intertribal warfare, a man was expected to give good horses, namely racing horses, to his brothers-in-law from time to time.

• Until recently, a family might negotiate to acquire a wife for a son by offering the girl's parents so many head of horses.

• When a family sponsors (adopts) a person into a ceremonial or social order, the adoptive parents would provide a fully outfitted horse for riding into the site where the event is held.

• Sometime after a marriage, the bride's parents would give a fully outfitted horse to the new son-in-law to ride in the big parade.

• In the pre-reservation days (before 1870 for the Crows), when a homicide occurred, accidentally or otherwise, the relatives of the deceased person would vow to take the life of the offender. Here, Keeper of the Peacepipe would intercede and arrange for a retribution offer of so many head of horses to the aggrieved family from the offender's relatives.

• In many of the giveaway events people would give horses to their clan fathers, to visitors from other districts, and even to friends from other tribes. It is often told, even to this day, that in the early 1900s the Big Horn District Crows gave more than four hundred horses to their visitors from the Lodge Grass District. Afterward the Big Horn District has been called Giveaway Valley.

Economic Life. In the early years of reservation life, a Crow man's wealth and economic status was measured by the number of horses he owned. One of the symbols of wealth was the ownership of many horses. (Having many relatives was another.)

Every Crow man aspired to own many horses. Until the Depression years of the 1930s, a man would sell his extra horses to horse buyers as a source of family income. The animals selected to be domesticated then constituted a man's occupation; he would work daily breaking horses to work or to ride and training thoroughbreds to run races. To be a Crow rancher in those days was to raise horses rather than cattle. Working with horses was regarded as more dignified than working with cattle only for the money; this prestige is another manifestation of the historical and cultural importance of the Crow Indian horse.

Finally, social customs involving frequent giving away of horses should be recognized as a system of circulation of wealth in the Crow economy.

WHAT HAS HAPPENED TO THE CROW INDIAN HORSES?

In 1882 the Crow tribe ceded the western portion of the vast Crow Indian Reservation to the United States and moved to the eastern sector. The Indians agents' new headquarters or agency was established in the Little Bighorn Valley about thirteen miles south of what is now Hardin, Montana, in 1884. The Crow families scattered to various areas of the diminished reservation, generally under the leadership of a chief or several chiefs. The main occupation of the Crow men was the traditional raising of and caring for horses, which was all they knew and enjoyed doing. During the Spanish-American War, the conflicts of the 1890s, and World War I, the Crow horse ranchers began to farm, raising garden produce, small grains, and hay for the horses. Family herds increased rapidly.

By the turn of the century, the number of horses the Crows owned was increasing rapidly, and by the end of World War I, the ranges were teeming with horses, which were becoming unmanageable and quite wild. By this time many non-Indian cattlemen and sheepmen had acquired grazing permits to large blocks of reservation land, and they were doing very well. They started complaining that wild Indian ponies were eating off their ranges, and some refused to pay their grazing fees. Before long these permittees and lessees, aided by Montana senators and congressmen, began pressuring the government to get rid of the Indian horses.

About 1919 the secretary of the interior issued orders that the Crows must get rid of their horses. This was like ordering a man to kill his best friend or brother. It was also ordering a people to relinquish the traditions, customs, and values of their culture, their way of life! Naturally, no Crow could abide by the secretary's orders. The ultimatum came about 1923, that the government would get rid of the horses. Local non-Indian cattle outfits were contracted to kill the horses on a bounty basis. The killer would be paid four dollars per animal when he produced the tip of a horse's ear. Some killers would bring in big sacks of ears. One large outfit had to import Texas gunmen to do the shooting, as local cowboys were soon disgusted with the slaughter. Of course, the Crows would not kill horses.

In a matter of three years nearly all the so-called wild mustangs were killed off. About one hundred head of the wildest ones were found in the rough Rotten Grass Breaks after World War II, and the same stockman who hired the Texas gunmen hired planes and helicopters and ran the poor horses to death. In the first slaughter the government said that about forty thousand head were exterminated, but the Crows said it was many more, including many tame ranch horses, which the gunmen preyed on when it got difficult to find wild ones.

Thus by 1930 the great and proud horse people, the Absarokee, were bereft of horses. When the horse was gone, the Crow culture was severely damaged. To say the least, this was a traumatic and tragic experience for a proud horse-oriented tribe; it was worse than actual military defeat, which some Plains tribes sustained.

The Northern Cheyenne tribe, whose reservation adjoined the Crow Reservation on the east, also suffered the same fate. A Cheyenne historian used to recall that a new Indian agent arrived for duty just before the onset of the horse slaughter. After surveying conditions on the reservation, he announced that the Cheyenne were in a sad state and that he would put them back on their feet as soon as possible. The agent did not speak with a forked tongue, the Cheyenne historian would add. Within a short time, all the Cheyenne horses were killed off and the Cheyenne were set on foot.

In 1934 John Collier was appointed Commissioner of Indian Affairs under the new Roosevelt Administration. When the Indian Reorganization Act was passed, Collier immediately launched his program to restructure the Indian Service, giving the tribes wide and generous latitude in managing their own reservation affairs. Corporate charters were issued to tribes accepting the new policy.

The commissioner appointed Robert Yellowtail, then forty-three years old, as the new superintendent of his own Crow Indian Reservation. Yellowtail was well educated and had taken a law course in California. He served as counsel and interpreter for Crow chiefs such as Plenty Coups and Medicine Crow in their many negotiations with the government over attempts by Montana senators and congressmen to open the Crow Reservation for homesteading by whites. Yellowtail knew how to deal with the whites.

The new superintendent immediately launched an ambitious program to rehabilitate his Crow people from the horse disaster, the ongoing drought, and the national Depression. The Crow people had to be economically and culturally invigorated! While taking advantage of the National Recovery Act programs, the superintendent also pursued long-range economic rehabilitation plans. His main goals were to restock the reservation with horses, as well as buffalo and elk. The buffalo program was quickly accomplished, as several hundred head of bison were donated by Yellowstone Park, by the National Bison Range of western Montana, and by some private individuals. To start the horse program, Yellowtail purchased and begged for registered stallions of various breeds and launched a full-scale breeding program. He named a Morgan stallion Roosevelt. This stallion sired many top calf-roping horses for Crow rodeo cowboys.

The Crow had lost his horses but not his love and ability to handle horses nor the importance he attached to horses in his culture. Former Crow horsemen enthusiastically joined the horse crusade, and before too long the horses were back. Lost concepts and values in Crow culture were revived.

With the resumption of the annual Crow Fair and Celebration after World War II, a steady demand grew for race horses, rodeo horses, parade horses, and just kid horses. With the easy availability of fine registered sires and mares in the country now, the Crow Indians have been increasing their herds with fine stock.

Today during the annual August tribal celebration, billed as the Tepee Capital of the World, attended by thousands of tribal people from throughout the United States and Canada, these fine modern Crow horses are to be seen by the hundreds in the daily parades through the camp, on the race track in the afternoon meets, and in the rodeo arena.

This is a sight to behold, truly a rare privilege to see, when hundreds of people, from tiny tots to octogenarians, pass in parade riding beautifully decorated mounts—a horse culture in action.

Thanks to Columbus for bringing the horse back to America!

From M.M.
to M.D.

From Medicine Man to Doctor of Medicine

The story of our ancestors is truly great, exciting, and worthy of retelling from time to time. We have been here in our Mother-Earth land—which the Europeans have called America, the New World, the Western Hemisphere—for a very long time.

The mountains, foothills, and valleys literally show the moccasin footprints of the Ancient Ones as they passed through here, camped in temporary rock shelters, sought visions on the peaks, or lived here for some time. Our tellers of stories and keepers of tribal annals can take us back into the past for only about four hundred years. Beyond that our histories quickly fade into the darkness of time. Here a new breed of storytellers, the modern archaeologists, take up the task of telling the stories of the Ancient Ones. Almost daily they enlighten us with new and interesting stories as they delve deeper and deeper into the long, long-ago times.

These archaeologists, armed with sophisticated chemical dating devices, now tell us that our predecessors have been here for some thirty to forty thousand years. As we stand here this day, we can boast and proudly proclaim membership in the oldest living race of mankind in the world.

So now, may I review a chapter in our proud racial history and tell when and where our ancestors did well. This is indeed a long story and cannot be told in one sitting. What follows at best may cover the preface, the introduction.

The title of this chapter is "From M.M. to M.D.," meaning "From Medicine Man to Doctor of Medicine." And in a broader sense, the title means "From Medicine Bundle to Doctor's Black Bag" or "From Medicine Lodge to PHS Hospital." These expressions attest to the Indian's achievements and progress in the art and science of healing the sick and treating the lame and to his contribution to the development of American, and world, medicine.

But before we get into the main story, terminology and semantic problems must be clarified. First, let us analyze what is meant by the terms *medicine, Indian medicine*, and, of course, *medicine man*. Webster's dictionary defines medicine as "a substance or preparation used in treating disease; something that affects well-being." In a broad sense, the dictionary recognizes medicine as "the science and art of preventing, alleviating, or curing disease." And in a specific sense, the dictionary defines medicine as "an object held by North American Indians to give control over natural or magical forces; also magical power and ritual."

It is this last definition describing Indian medicine only in terms of the magical, mystical, and the ritualistic that concerns and perhaps disturbs many Indians today. No doubt Christian settlers who regarded the natives of this new world as savages and heathens first formed this concept, and it has been perpetuated by the ethnocentric white man ever since. In fact, the expressions medicine and Indian medicine are white-men's words as surely as papoose, squaw, tomahawk, tom-tom, and many others.

So we ask, what is the white man trying to say when he describes something as having good medicine or bad medicine, having strong or poor medicine? And when he says "medicine," is he talking about a buckskin pouch containing healing herbs or containing objects representing certain mysterious and supernatural powers? And who or what is this person the white man likes to call medicine man or shaman? Is he talking about a man earnestly treating and healing the sick, lame, and wounded, or is he talking about a man using ritual and ceremony in making a prophecy, dealing with a severe natural happening, or solving a great mystery confronting the people?

It is all confusing, isn't it? I think the only way to clarify the situation is to ask and find out how the Indians themselves name, explain, and describe these things. With the Indians the term *medicine* embraces much more than the curing of diseases and the healing of injuries. It includes that which is mysterious, holy, sacred, and supernatural. The Sioux have a nice word for it, *Wakan*, as did some eastern tribes in the word *Manitou*.

The central and formal aspects of Indian medicine were ceremonial in nature. As such, then, the healing arts of the Indian were, and still are, an integral part of his religion. To the Indian, medicine and religion are closely interwoven and knitted together: One is an integral part of the other; one cannot function without the other. It is almost impossible to tell where practical healing ends and ceremonial healing begins. Matters get complicated when the always pesky art of magic enters the picture.

To be sure, the tribes of North America had a wide variety of religions and healing systems. Some of the more primitive tribes had but one medical and religious practitioner who handled all the healing tasks of the tribe by himself. In the more advanced, sedentary, and agricultural tribes, there were many specialist healers, professional priests, and healing societies. Their functions ranged from simple treatment of sick and injured individuals to holding complex and highly sophisticated ceremonials that dealt with the welfare and well-being of entire tribal populations.

There was, however, one thing that tribes held, more or less, in common. This concerned the attitude, concept, and philosophy of the *cause* and *cure* of diseases. In general, North American tribes classed disease by cause rather than by symptom, the part of the body affected, or any other characteristic. It seemed that they were primarily concerned with *why* a person was sick or hurt rather than with what the sickness or injury was all about.

These causes were identified and listed under two categories: the natural and the supernatural. Naturally caused diseases and illnesses were such things as complications from childbirth, broken bones, wounds from warfare or encounters with animals, and accidents; death in early childhood and death from old age were also considered natural. Supernaturally caused diseases and afflictions were such things as bad luck due to breaking taboos, loss of soul, possession by evil spirits, intrusion of a foreign object into the body, and effects of witchcraft or black magic.

The method of treating and curing the sick, injured, and afflicted depended on the type of cause diagnosed. The treatment of naturally caused ailments involved practical knowledge of physical manipulations and techniques such as heat treatments, cauterization, bone-setting, sutures, poultices, and so on, and also the use of time-proven and usually dependable medicinal herbs. The treatment of supernaturally caused ailments and afflictions was a much more serious and complicated affair. Any one of the causes already mentioned could create a large number of symptoms and complications, to use a modern medical term; thus, professional diagnosis was necessary.

And this brings us face to face with the so-called medicine man. So we ask again who and what was this individual called "medicine man" by the white man, *Wicasa Wakan* by the Sioux, *Batce Baxbe* by the Crow, and other names by other tribes? To be sure, he was not always an Indian. Primitive men of all races, ages, and parts of the world had them. This medicine man, or better, man of medicine, was both born and made. He was born of supernatural circumstances and made of natural circumstances.

First, we ask how was he made? He was made over thousands of centuries of gastronomical experimentation with unknown plants. Some killed him and some cured him, of course, but then he came through with good and practical knowledge of herbs that were best suited for relieving and curing his aches and pains. This was the practitioner who generally first handled the common ailments and injuries diagnosed to be caused by natural things and circumstances. He was the specialist who knew by training what herbs to prescribe for toothaches, skin troubles, insect and snake bites, broken ankles, wounds, and other common and external ailments.

Next, we ask how was he born to be a medicine man? There comes a time in the lives of people (family group, clan, band, tribe) when an event, or a series of happenings, disrupts the ordinary, routine, and usual ways of doing things and living. The people are not able to explain it; they can't straighten things out, or they are powerless to do anything about it all. This, then, is the time when the people start wondering, guessing, and finally blaming the bad state of affairs on an outside cause, some big force or forces beyond the realm of the natural. Here—as men seek and attempt to influence, guard, regulate, and control the supernatural force or power causing all the troubles and to establish a better working relationship—the medicine man is born!

With his innate intelligence and other capabilities, which are perhaps more acute, sensitive, and responsive than in other people, the medicine man comes up with a definition of the situation and a solution. To be sure, he does not come up with an instant answer. He must go through a period of soul-searching, propitiation, and vision seeking; ultimately he must experience a holy communion with the Great Power and gain spiritual insight and wisdom in the ways of the Great Spirit. It is then known that this man can receive power and use it to help his people in sickness and distress.

Thus, he becomes the man, the special one, who can use supernatural powers to diagnose the cause of serious ailments, injuries, and wounds, and he is able to prescribe the right treatment and cure. He becomes the man who is able to diagnose the cause of a great tribulation threatening his people and to invoke the appropriate ceremonial procedure to solve or otherwise relieve and release the people from the situation. He can look into the future and foretell or prophesy coming events, good or bad. If bad, he is able to avoid or circumvent the impending threat.

There were medicine men and medicine men, which is to say that there were divisions, classes, and ranks in this profession. These were, of course, arranged differently from tribe to tribe and from culture area to culture area, but they were basically the same.

One thing is sure. This unusual and interesting individual was more than just the white man's stereotyped image of a character in weirdo costumes and paraphernalia, brandishing rattles and feathers, muttering unintelligible grunts, chanting invocations, and jumping and hovering over a poor sick and scared person. More often he is depicted as deceiving his patient or subject with trickery and sleight of hand. It is said that he lived and thrived by imposing on the credulity of those who depended on him and by asking exorbitant fees.

On the contrary, the average Indian medical or holy man was a decent sort, hardworking, sincere, aware of the seriousness of his responsibilities, and dedicated to the individual well-being and general welfare of his people and community. It is indeed unfortunate that the true image of this indispensable man of the tribe and his genuine and great contributions have been so long belittled, tarnished, and obscured by the ethnocentric white man.

Now in coming to the last pages of this chapter of our story, let me hurriedly describe the usual and general arrangement and classification that the Northern Plains Indians used in describing their medical and holy men engaged in the healing and problem-solving business. The following order of arrangement is based primarily on the seriousness of the ailment or situation involved and the caliber of treatment thus called for:

1. Nonprofessionals using simple and commonly known home remedies in treating simple ailments and injuries, equivalent to first-aid treatment. It was usually the wise old

grandmother who treated the immediate members of the family as part of her daily chores.

2. General practitioners treating minor ailments and injuries with practical therapeutics and well-known medicinal or healing herbs. These people might treat any patient and might or might not accept remuneration for their services. They did their job without fanfare.

3. Professional specialists who treated only certain serious and obstinate diseases, injuries, and afflictions believed or diagnosed to be caused by supernatural agents. They used special compounds whose formulas were known only to them, and they also used ritual and ceremony. Such a personality received his power from supernatural beings or agents during a vision quest. They asked for set or special fees.

4. Holy men who dealt exclusively in nonbodily afflictions believed to be caused by supernatural agents, such as dangerous events threatening the people, famine, severe weather, etc. These men depended upon and used a full ceremonial or religious approach. The men in this category asked for no material compensation, receiving instead the gratitude, respect, and allegiance of their people. These men were usually head chiefs and men of high rank.

5. Prophets and visionaries who were concerned and responsible for the welfare of war parties and hunting parties, as well as the entire community. These men could foretell important coming events and advise what action to take. Like representatives of the previous category, these were generally head chiefs and men of high rank who asked no compensation for their services other than the gratitude, respect, and allegiance of the people.

In addition to these five classes, some tribes had healing societies or organizations—variously named the Medicine

Lodge, the Wound-Healing Order, and so on—that ministered to all forms of illness, injury, and community problem. These organizations used group consultation and participation, and elaborate ceremony was utilized involving singing, dancing, and other activities.

Then there is a class of pseudo–medicine men who resorted to and utilized trickery and false means. In general these practitioners used magic, sorcery, and witchcraft. They could do good or evil: They too could treat sickness and find lost articles, horses, and even humans; they could prescribe love medicine. But they also cast spells and curses on their fellow men; they could become false prophets.

Now I ask myself how can I bring to a close the retelling of this chapter of the Indian story on a fitting note? Certainly we Indians have developed our medicine bundles into large medical cabinets and storage rooms full of powerful drugs and sophisticated medical instruments. It is said that no fewer than a hundred and seventy Indian-proven medicinal herbs and plants have been accepted and added to the official U.S. Pharmacopeia and the National Formulary.

And certainly our M.M.'s (medicine men) can and have metamorphosed into full-fledged modern M.D.'s. I understand there are today about forty-five Indian physicians occupying high positions in the medical profession throughout the United States, about twenty-seven medical students, and a host of premeds.

Our story "From M.M. to M.D." has been good, and let us hope that it will get better and better.

The Crow Fair

~~~~~~~~~~~~~~~~~~~~~~~

Um-basax-bilua is what the Crow Indians call their annual Crow Fair, held the third week of August. Those words literally mean "where they make the noise." Sometimes the event is referred to as the "Tepee Capital of the World."

In 1904, S. C. Reynolds, the government Indian agent assigned to the Crow Reservation in south-central Montana, conceived the county fair idea as one of the means by which the Crow Indians could be induced to become farmers and eventually to become self-supporting. He planned the project as a typical county fair, then popular in the midwestern section of the United States. He hoped that exhibiting the produce raised by neophyte Indian farmers at the tribal fair would encourage them to become better and better farmers. Reynolds also arranged for Indian women to exhibit processed native foods as well as handcrafts. Winners in the various categories received ribbons and cash prizes.

For the social and entertainment aspects of the fair, Agent Reynolds relaxed the government's strict policy of forbidding Indians to conduct traditional dances, ceremonials, singing, and other "Indian doings." He apparently reasoned that dispensing with the restrictions during the fair would encourage the people to participate and make the new venture a success. He therefore set up a committee of old chiefs and elders to come up with a schedule of entertainment events. The committee quickly made arrangements for morning parades, afternoon foot and horse racing, and evening dancing. Several "town criers" were selected to do the announcing. The agent approved the schedule.

The first year the new event was held in an open meadow about two miles south of the Custer Battlefield. The following year a one-half-mile racetrack and an exhibit hall were built. Also, during the gathering medium-size circus tents were set up for the districts to hold their evening dances.

Within a few years Reynolds's dream had become a reality, as nearly all families of the six districts of the reservation began farming and raising livestock in earnest. At fair time the new farmers would bring in their farm produce and livestock to exhibit and show. Before long the women started exhibiting their processed native foods and costumes of buckskin and beads that they had made during the winter. Horseback-riding paraphernalia were popular exhibit items. Boys would bring pet ponies and calves to show; some brought chickens and turkeys.

The old chiefs and elders, true pre-reservation Crows, took advantage of the agent's relaxation of the strict rules and heightened the festive mood of the gathering with sham battles, reenactments of events from the former days of intertribal warfare, victory dances, public recitals of war deeds by veteran warriors, and gift distributions to clan relatives, thus reviving rituals heretofore prohibited by the government.

By 1920 the afternoon events at the racetrack were expanded to include wrestling, tepee-erection races, rodeo events, and even dancing exhibitions by renowned dancers of the tribe.

During World War I, the drought and Depression years of the 1930s, and World War II, the annual fairs were canceled. When the event was resumed after World War II, the agricultural exhibits were forgotten. Nearly all Indian farmers quit farming during the drought and Depression and worked instead for the WPA, CCC, or other New Deal programs.

The festive features of the fair, however, not only survived but flourished, growing bigger and better. The spirit of competition in agricultural efforts so cherished by S. C. Reynolds was replaced by competition in parades, horsemanship, and entertainment. Today cash awards are given to winners in various categories of the parade—best-dressed man, best-dressed woman, best-dressed boys and girls. Cash prizes are also given for the best-decorated pickup truck, passenger car, and large float. Fierce competition at the modern Crow Fair makes the morning parades the most spectacular and colorful Indian parade in America.

Today the format of the fair consists of six days of morning parades, early morning "slack time" rodeo, afternoon horse races and rodeo, late-afternoon dancing contests for the children, and evening powwow dancing in the huge arbor. The fifth day is reserved for the host Crow tribe to conduct the "Dancing Through the Camp" ritual. Symbolism based on the sacred number four is used freely during the performance by way of praying for a good year until the people gather again the following August. Four leaders are selected to lead the participants in a long procession around the main sector of the encampment. At each of four designated stops a leader tells a good-luck or good-deed story and prays that the people will have similar good experiences during the coming year. Here four songs are sung by the drummers, and the procession moves on to the next stop. The fourth and final stop is made inside the dancing arbor.

At this point the officials of the Um-basax-bilua take over. Each official presents gifts to tribal elders, visitors, and special clan relatives to show appreciation for having been selected to manage this huge undertaking. It is the Crow custom that an honoree gives away presents, instead of receiving presents as non-Indians do.

The final or sixth day is also special to the Crows. At this time the outgoing officials provide a big feast for all. Afterward, officers for the next Crow Fair are elected.

Fair week at Crow Agency, Montana, is truly all-American—a combination county or state fair, a large horse race featuring twelve contests per day, a huge modern rodeo where about seven hundred Indian cowboys compete, and daily parades of horseback riders and decorated vehicles sometimes two miles long. And, of course, at the Crow Fair one can see the largest tepee camp in the world, where at least seven hundred and as many as one thousand tepees are pitched in neat rows around a conglomerate of three camp circles. Such a camp is indeed a sight to behold, not only for non-Indians but for modern Indians themselves.

The English meaning of Um-basax-bilua ("where they make the noise") is an accurate description of today's Crow Fair and Celebration. When twenty to thirty thousand Indians from Canada and the United States camp together, a whole lot of noise prevails. Twenty to thirty singing groups sing and beat the drums over powerful sound amplifiers; hundreds of dancers with bells tied to their ankles pound the dance floor; camp criers ride through the camp in sound cars making announcements. Extraneous noise comes from thousands of kids whooping and screaming, dogs barking, horses neighing, bikers revving their motors, and even helicopters roaring overhead as they fly sightseers around!

The modern Crow Fair and Celebration is much more than dancing, horse racing, and rodeoing. It is a big family reunion; Crow Indians living in the various parts of the large reservation camp together to visit, feast, and recount old family stories and history. It is a time when members of other tribes come to visit their Crow friends. Many non-Indians come to look, take pictures, and move on; others come purposely to participate in the various activities. Europeans, mainly members of "Indian clubs" in Germany, France, and England, come to live like real Indians for a week. There is joy, friendliness, and even frivolity throughout the camp!

But in a more serious way the Crow Um-basax-bilua is a time of cultural renewal, a time to display the Crow culture in action. This annual event is the time to tell the world that Crow Indians of Montana have a strong cultural persistence worthy of emulation by other tribes of all the Americas!

Crow Indian Humor

Jokes, Jests, and Anecdotes

ontrary to the general impression that Indians are stoical, unsmiling, and stone-faced, Indians are, in fact, full of humor and hilarity among themselves. At powwows men from different tribes visit and exchange new jokes and funny stories, and before long the same joke is told all over the Indian country.

In the old pre-reservation days, the main form of Crow Indian humor was the singing of jesting songs. Rival warrior societies would compose songs about each other's anecdotes, eccentricities, and breaking certain clan taboos, such as a man's mentioning the name of his mother-in-law.

Today this form of humor has been replaced by what is called "telling about one's ways." This particular form of humor is not used indiscriminately. Only the Opposites (children of patrilineal clans) may use it to tease, ridicule, and castigate one another publicly. These Opposites, some-times called "teasing clans," have the license to watch one another, and they are quick to fabricate outrageous tales about one another's ways. People enjoy these humorous tales, and before long these incredible stories become true.

Today tribal people tell jokes and humorous stories about themselves and laugh at themselves. Life on reservations, with high unemployment, alcoholism, and poor health, is often harsh. Indian humor stories provide an outlet for frustrations. People "roll with the punch" with these grin- and laugh-provoking stories. There are, however, some militant and activist Indians who object to these stories as "racial jokes," but as a whole the reservation Indians not only tolerate but enjoy listening to and telling these stories.

Here are a few stories Indians tell about one another.

THE DAY BIG SHEEP GOT THE BEST OF BILL LYNDE, A SHREWD HORSE TRADER

This is a true story, which happened near the little reservation town of Lodge Grass, Montana, back in the 1930s. The story has been around. Even Paul Harvey told a white-man's version recently.

Big Sheep lived about two miles up Lodge Grass Creek from the town of Lodge Grass, Montana. His neighbor was called the Slim White Man, but his real name was Bill Lynde. (He was the grandfather of Stan Lynde, the Montana cartoonist.) The Slim White Man was a professional horse trader, seldom a loser. But one day Big Sheep got the best of him with only three words of English.

Big Sheep was preliterate, but he had picked up a lot of white-man talk while playing cards at the pool hall. He was adept at playing "dumb Indian," but actually he was "dumb like a fox." One day he decided to trade off to the Slim One a horse that was blind in one eye. After grooming the old bay a bit, he got on and headed to his neighbor's place. Slim White Man was sitting in the shade of his barn and whittling when Big Sheep went by on his prancing bay. Slim looked over the passerby and hollered to Big Sheep to come over. But Big Sheep merely shook his head and answered, "Me go fin' em ponies." He went on.

After a while Big Sheep came back, with his bay still prancing and looking real sharp. This time the horse trader was waiting by the gate. He invited his neighbor to get off and have some coffee. And before long he made his pitch.

"Big Sheep, you have good pony."

"Yah, heap good," replied Big Sheep.

"Maybe you trade, heh?"

"Maybe no."

The negotiations picked up as Bill Lynde said, "I'll tell you what I'll do, I will trade you my good grey, the one you liked."

Big Sheep did not reply but appeared interested.

Bill repeated, "I will give you the grey and this ten-dollar bill for poker money."

Big Sheep then executed his play: "Slim, you good white man; you good friend and me like you heap good. But this pony don't look good." In the Crow language the word for "look" and "see" is the same.

The Slim One smiled and said, "Big Sheep, this horse doesn't look too bad. Is it a deal?"

Whereupon Big Sheep got off his horse, unsaddled it, and walked over to the grey. He saddled up and rode off without a word.

The next morning the shrewd one who seldom lost came over to Big Sheep's place and accosted him. "Hey, Big

Sheep, you have forked tongue. You didn't tell me that this bay is blind in one eye. You are crooked."

With his finest expression of innocence, Big Sheep replied, "Me tellem you this horse 'don't look good.' "

Bill Lynde, who knew enough Crow language, concluded that he'd been taken. He turned and left without another word to Big Sheep, but he muttered some profanity as he walked away.

THE EDUCATED YOUNG INDIAN AND HIS UNEDUCATED OLD GRANDFATHER

This story could have taken place on any Indian reservation in the early twentieth century. A young man, who had been away several years attending a government school, came back to the reservation. He didn't hide his disdain for reservation life. He felt that with his education he was superior to the reservation Indians, especially the old people who could not write, read, or speak the English language.

John, let's call him, and his old grandfather didn't strike it off from the beginning. When Grandpa and others talked to John, he would pretend that he didn't understand the tribal language. It wasn't long before the old man was convinced that the boy was ashamed to be an Indian. He was also sure that his grandson was so educated in the whiteman's ways that he was unfit and helpless to live on an Indian ranch. He couldn't chop firewood, build a fire, hitch harnesses on horses, or do any other routine work.

John would often harangue his grandpa, saying that his problem was that he was always looking back to his so-called good old days, the buffalo hunting and war party days. He was not facing the realities of modern life.

The grandfather would retort that John's problem was

that he thought he was so smart, but actually he was dumb in ordinary ways of life.

There was indeed a lack of communication between the two, the young and the old, the educated and the uneducated. They couldn't talk in the same language nor see the same things.

Finally one day Grandpa remarked, "Since you think you are so smart, what did you study and learn in the big school?"

"Grandpa," John answered, "in reply to your academic inquiry, may I inform you that I matriculated at Carlisle Institute and majored in math. That is short for mathematics."

"Then say something in ma, ma, math, or whatever."

"I shall simply quote an equation in algebra," the grandson said. "Pi r squared equals . . ."

"Hold it, hold it right there," the grandfather interrupted. "Say that again real slow."

"Pi r squared equals . . ."

"I know it! I know it all the time that you are plumb dumb! Any old fool knows that pies are not square. Pies are round!" Grandpa shook his head and walked off as John tried to explain.

Later John suggested to Grandpa that the next time he got a lease check they go to the big city. There he would show Grandpa the wonders of the white-man's civilization.

One day they got on the train and headed for the big city, probably Denver. John took his grandfather to the city center, where the tall buildings reached into the sky, where large stores lined the avenues, and where they dodged automobiles and trolleys as they crossed streets. Grandpa looked all around but didn't say anything.

They visited an art gallery. They came to the painting *End of the Trail,* which shows an Indian and his horse bending forward, ready to fall into a chasm. John explained that when a white-man artist paints a picture, he tells a story, the meaning of the picture. In this painting the artist is telling the story of the Indian race: The Indian and his way of life have come to the end. The Indian and his horse, which represents his Plains Indian culture, are about to fall into the bottomless canyon and disappear. "In other words, Grandpa, you are that old and tired Indian on the horse. What have you to say?"

Grandpa looked at his grandson for a long time and then, pointing a finger at him and then at the painting, said, "That Indian is you and all other young 'educated' youths who drink and drive a sick horse about ready to crash!"

The two walked back to the railroad depot in silence, each no doubt thinking he had won the argument.

THE INDIAN COWBOY

After World War II rodeo became a great pastime on the various reservations throughout the Indian country. In between the so-called all-Indian rodeos, many Indian rodeo cowboys would go to county-fair rodeos and other off-reservation rodeos.

The story goes that several boys from a reservation in South Dakota formed a team and would go rodeoing all summer. One day after the rodeo the boys sat around and talked about their performance. Then one of them said to the bareback rider Joe Stinks: "Joe, you just gotta change your name. The rodeo announcers joke about your name, sometimes saying that your ride was a 'stinker' and all that. As it is, the whites like to make fun of our names and tend to look down at us."

One day they practically forced Joe to go to the county courthouse and have his name changed legally. Soon he was on the road hitchhiking. But before long he was back, saying that it would take twenty-five bucks to make a name change.

After a good day at a rodeo the boys chipped in and gave Joe twenty-five dollars. He left and came back the next day all smiles. The boys surrounded him, curious to know if he had selected a good white-man's name, like Jones, Smith, or Johnson. He just smiled and told them to listen to the announcer. They would hear his new name just before he was to come out of the chute on the horse called W. O. Grey.

Finally there was only one more rider to come out. The announcer cleared his throat and boomed over the sound system: "Ladies and gentlemen, we have a real treat for you! The bucking horse of the year, W. O. Grey, is now in chute number six. And the cowboy on him will be JOE STINKS NO MORE!"

The audience howled, but the group of Indian cowboys standing against the arena fence moaned, "Oh, no."

THE INDIAN COWBOY'S BRAIN

Here is another Indian cowboy story. Indian listeners get a big kick out of it, but sometimes a militant will take exception to the story as a racial joke.

There was a seminar where marketing experts from medical supply firms came to promote their products. One salesman representing a firm that supplied transplantable human organs brought three containers of brains. He pointed to one and explained that the brain once belonged to a skilled neurosurgeon. Unfortunately, the doctor was killed in an auto accident, but his brain was saved and was now ready to be used. The price? The price was eight hundred dollars. He pointed to another container and said that the brain once belonged to a top NASA rocket scientist. The asking price, he added, was nine hundred dollars. The third brain, he went on to explain, once belonged to an Indian cowboy. The price for it was two thousand dollars.

There was a hush and then a big stir in the audience. Finally a man asked, "Sir, how can you ask so much for the brain of an ordinary Indian, a cowboy at that?"

The salesman quickly replied, "Why, sir, this brain is like new! It has hardly been used at all! It will be good for many, many years."

THE DRINKING MAN'S FOUR WISHES

This story has a moral to it; in fact, there are two. I have often used this fable when I speak to Indian students and at gatherings of Indian youth. The first moral lesson is about the usually high rate of unemployment on Indian reservations, and the second is about being one's own self and not trying to be somebody else.

The setting of this story could be anywhere in the Indian country where the main town is situated just outside the boundary of the reservation. One summer day a young man stirred from his sleep. The sun was already quite high and the day started out hot. George Short Bull's head was splitting, his mouth was dry, and his hands were shaking. He was in bad shape! His first thought was to get a quick drink, an eye-opener to calm his nerves. He ventured onto the main street, but the town was really dead this time of the morning.

He figured there was no use trying to panhandle for drinking money, so he decided to hitchhike back to the "res" and perhaps "borrow" his grandfather's powwow dancing outfit to hock at the pawn shop or sell to the bootlegger on the south side of the railroad.

On his way along the highway, George would pick up any bottle or beer can to see if there was a little stuff left in it. Soon he forgot about hitchhiking and started looking for bottles in earnest. Then he spotted a fifth bottle of a high-priced whiskey. The label read: "Four Roses, 100 Proof." No doubt it had been thrown out of a big Cadillac or Continental by one of the rich ranchers who lease Indian land. The bottle was made of dark glass, and George couldn't see if there was anything in it, so he slowly unscrewed the cap, and out popped a genie, a little Indian genie girl all dressed up in a fancy shawl dance outfit. She had in her hand a feather fan, her wishing wand.

Genie said: "Make four wishes and all will come true."

George Short Bull: "You ain't pulling my leg, are you?"

Genie: "Go ahead with your first wish."

George thought about his need for money to get a quick drink and replied: "Okay, first I need some hard cash." The little "medicine girl" waved her feather wand and pointed to a briefcase, a really fancy one such as the kind Indian politicians carry to D. C. on tribal business.

George opened the case. There neatly bundled and stacked were brand-new greenbacks, some tens, twenties, thirties, even thousands. He fingered the bills and let out a loud war whoop.

Genie asked George for his second wish.

George, now feeling good and smiling big, muttered: "Let's see. With all this dough I've got to have transportation. I need a car to go to powwows and rodeos and to give the girls rides."

Another wave of the wand and there, parked in front of

George, was a long, sleek, black Cad with glistening bumpers, grille, and side trimmings. He climbed in and looked at the fancy dashboard. He pushed a button; out blared music, loud but smooth. He turned another knob, and now the music was the latest powwow song, which fancy dancers liked.

The little medicine girl interrupted the singing and asked George for his third wish. This time he took his time, thinking about making the right wish. He looked at the briefcase full of money, looked at the fancy Cad, and then looked at himself in the rearview mirror. He saw a tough-looking character wearing dirty clothes and mismatched sneakers. Then he came up with a good one: "With all my money and a snazzy car to snag the ladies, I've just gotta look neat and sharp so the gals will flock after me. Now, my third wish is to be real handsome, wearing terrific clothes. Make me look like Burt Reynolds or Elvis."

The wand waved the third time, and there stood a real dude! His sports jacket was white with glittering pink and green sequins, his pink shirt was unbuttoned way down low. He looked down to see his alligator boots tipped with silver and gold. He was wearing a real John B. Stetson hat, something like George Straight's hat.

As he was admiring himself and grinning wide, the genie said it was time for his final wish; she cautioned George to be very careful.

George Short Bull: "With all this, especially the money, fix it, Little One, so I'll never have to worry about finding a job and going to work."

Pop, and the genie disappeared.

George Short Bull was back to his Indian self.

Index

134